Finding myself with Parkinson's

Ludwig has had a nagging pain in his right shoulder for a few days. Wrong move? Or sore muscle?

A few months later, it turned out the pain marked the onset of Parkinson's disease.

On the cusp of his fiftieth birthday, Ludwig seemed to have it all: he was blessed with a loving family and a successful career as an entrepreneur. But the diagnosis hit and upended his life. Faced with a huge personal challenge – his first - he analyzed the drastic changes in his body, mind, and heart.

In this witty and offbeat fiction inspired by a true story, the author takes us from the initial bewilderment through the long process of learning to accept the mystifying condition and its army of little-known symptoms.

An account that challenges our own approach to illness, whether it impacts us or our loved ones.

With this guilt-free, touching, and fun read, the author hopes to turn a scary word into an invitation to seize the moment and its gifts.

<u>PREFACE</u>

Can one write about Parkinson's without scaring off potential readers?

I will venture a Yes to this question, based on the many testimonials I have received from readers who, overcoming their fear of the disease, chose to proceed through my book and share with me the interest, comfort, even hope they have gained from it.

When *Fifty-one* was published, it came to live a life of its own atop living-room coffee tables or displayed as an e-book on tablet screens. It occupied readers' minds for a few hours, called for their attention, got them thinking, wondering, comparing. It sparked enthusiasm, perhaps, or curiosity, or even indifference.

It has been critiqued and reviewed, seen on TV, discussed on the radio, picked up by journalists. It has carved out its own little niche amidst the vast ocean of literary releases.

It draws pride and courage from its first months of existence, in turn pleasing, moving, enlightening, intriguing, amusing, entertaining.

And so it goes on its merry way, giving its author a chance to thumb his nose at the aches and pains caused by the despotic and invasive intruder that has been creeping up on him.

1. <u>CLICK</u>

*Ksar Massa on the south coast of Morocco, 4:48 am –
June 2007*

Click. The shutter snaps the picture.

Hasni the photographer gestures at the fifty-or-so
people gathered before him: they are free to go. Most
are dressed in white djellabas bought for the occasion in
a souk for tourists.

They did a lot of talking, drinking, laughing, and dancing.

They are tired but happy with the change of scenery.
The sun has finally risen from beyond the desert
mountains encircling their hotel. They have gotten into
the habit of ending their yearly seminars with an all-
nighter before flying back to Paris, and this one is no
exception.

The return flight to CDG airport is bound to pass in a
flash as fatigue washes over the wearied revelers. Soon,

too soon, they will land, and resume work the next day, fulfilling their assignment as best they can.

In consultant-speak, one doesn't work, one is on assignment. Consultants don't have managers, they have collaborators. They set up office at the clients and don't see much of each other during the year.

Hence, this late June convention is a great opportunity for them to get together or meet for the first time. It's a recipe for success: magnificent vistas of the Counter-Atlas and the Atlantic, fishermen's villages, endless sandy beaches, fun and games, swimming, all in a lively atmosphere with actual work reduced to a minimum.

A man with white-blond hair stands out in the group photo. He is also wearing a djellaba, only his is black. The satisfaction that show through his reserved smile signals he is enjoying the moment.

He and his business partners have recruited over a hundred consultants since founding the firm less than five years ago. They work with major banks and have built a solid reputation as Banking process transformation experts– a profession that sounds foreign to most people.

Soon after he had created it, he sold his first firm for a substantial sum thanks to the Internet bubble – enough to keep him free from want for a few years. As it turns out, he has never lacked for life's necessities.

He sails back to his room for a short night. There – he empties his pockets, pulls out a key, a card holder, and a small piece of rolled-up paper. He smiles: the group leaders had written something akin to a prophecy on each paper roll, the kind one finds in fortune cookies. The one he picked at dinner earlier reads: "Get ready for a life-changing encounter". The game concocted by the group leaders entails stating your "future" out loud; when a young trainee drew the same prophecy and read it aloud to the other dinner guests, the banter flew thick and fast.

He will be home soon, back in the beautiful apartment he recently moved into with his wife and four children. He can't wait to be reunited with them again.

For the past few years, reality kept pace with his dreams– and more. He sees it as a just reward for all his hard work, with just a bit of luck thrown in for good measure.

He is friendly and warm, compassionate even. People like him. Aware of his success, he doesn't brag about it. Still, he can't help feeling somewhat invincible now, after years of low self-esteem.

To be totally honest, there is a hint of false modesty in his attitude that can be a bit grating at times, especially since he seems to have trouble understanding other people's problems.

He knows he is privileged, and he would simply like to keep it that way.

***

She wasn't in the picture. She has been waiting for him; there he is, at last. He looks tired. His lightly tanned skin contrasts with his fair hair. He tells her about his seminar, especially the best parts. She goes over what she did while he was away, throwing in a few anecdotes. She had helped him choose an outfit for the offbeat skit session before he left. As it turns out, the Alsatian headdress he borrowed from his mother was a big hit. She is happy for him. It is a shame she couldn't be there to see it – it must have been great fun.

She can't help brooding over the fact that she stayed in Paris while he was abroad enjoying himself. Okay, it's not that bad, but she could have done with a change of scene. She loves him, they live a comfortable life. In fact, they have more than they need. More than she has ever asked for. She even feels guilty about it sometimes– she wasn't raised in such abundance. It's as if she were living his life rather than her own. She longs for them to share a closer bond.

He thinks she is fulfilled. After all, don't they have four beautiful children, whom she raises with infinite love and care? She takes great pleasure in dressing them as she dreams for them. She likes fabrics, cuts, colors, patterns. A few years back, she would spend hours designing clothes. She was talented– but it's a thing of the past now. She misses it.

And yet she gets to travel a lot, she goes on holidays, she throws parties, she buys things… what is there for her to complain about? He, for one, can't see why she would. He knows her life hasn't always been easy. She suffered a loss in her youth that left her with a gaping void. He thinks their marriage and children have helped her move on, but he is mistaken. She can't move on.

She senses his annoyance at her sudden bouts of melancholy, her long phone conversations with her friends Lorelei and Joy, or her afternoons with Smith's mother Kate. Smith and their second son Antonin are friends. He would probably like to see her take control of her life and be more active, but her unease runs deeper than that. She expects more from him, she needs him to encourage her, boost her, and above all help her feel more confident about herself. But, instead of "pushing her out there", he insists on protecting her.

While they seem so happy on the outside, she sometimes wonders how much he really loves her. Whenever she says, "I love you", he tells her he loves her too. But he is never the one to say it first.

***

He asks her about her weekend, about her job, about the kids, about her mother. He is happy to take her in his arms. Last night is receding into a distant memory. Locked eyes. Intertwined laughter. Inhibitions loosened by alcohol.

He looks at her. He loves her. He would like her to be happier. He makes a joke or two. She smiles. He cannot see that he may just be hindering her, unwittingly, simply by being who he is. He never really thought about it. As far as he is concerned, he is making an effort to "put himself in her shoes".

A phrase that sounds like a promise, albeit one that's hard to keep.

***

A few hours earlier, in Agadir: The seminar host is at his wits' end. His team failed to check that all the consultants had actually boarded the departure bus, and now one of the most brilliant consultants, Clara, is nowhere to be found. He calls the photographer, who is still at the hotel packing his gear, and asks him to have a look around and make sure everyone is gone. Where is she? he wonders with mounting anxiety.

The photographer hangs up. As he raises his phone to take a selfie, a young woman's face appears onscreen. She nestles against his shoulder and draws her lips close to his. She was about to be promoted from senior to manager, but she doesn't care anymore. While he captured her beaming face earlier, in the darkroom, she unrolled her fortune-telling paper. It read: "Lightning never strikes twice". They saw it as a sign.

Whereas the seminar was nothing more than a break to most of their colleagues, it upended their lives. Click. That's it. The lens has landed them on reel for good.

2. <u>DOUBLE-CLICK</u>

Paris, 4:48 am, a morning like any other – September 2017

It's early. Way too early.

Awakened against his will by the incongruous and untimely contraction of the muscles in his back immediately followed by an even more crippling cramp in his third toe, he has no choice but to get up. Groggy and barely awake, he slips out of bed as quietly as possible so as not to disturb Aure, lying in blissful slumber next to him.

In the long corridor that leads to the kitchen, he drags his sleepy feet along the bow window overlooking the galvanized roofs of the 'Musée d'Orsay'. He walks to the sink, opens a drawer, rummages for a foil strip. The Sinemet tablet wrapped inside has the same effect on him as Inca gold on Spanish conquistadors. Catching his unkempt reflection in the anodized aluminum, he pops out a blue tablet and swallows it at once.

He knows it will be at least an hour before the drug takes effect. With feet like lead, he shuffles to the living room and falls into the chair in front of his computer. Keen to resume typing his text, he enters his password. Next comes the double-click, a simple gesture that has become an automatic reflex for billions of his fellow earthlings – but not for him. Having to press and release the mouse button twice in rapid succession brings him back to his new condition: no matter how hard he tries to control his index finger; it seems to live a life of its own. After many failed attempts, he somehow manages to tap an acceptable "double-click" that is immediately rewarded with a window opening onto the vast world.

***

Maousse's wake-up call is harsh too. As with every morning, the desk light came on without warning. Yesterday it woke him at 6:10, today at 4:53, and tomorrow... who knows?

He should have slept longer; his eyes are bloodshot, and his face is drawn from lack of sleep. The part of his brain governing his writing skills seems to be the only one in working order, as it guides his numb fingers over the keyboard.

"He should really go back to bed, he's in no condition to write."

The letters change into words as they progress along the page. Tentative at first, they gain confidence, gradually steadying their sporadic pace, and soon get so bold that they start anticipating Double-Click's imagination.

The way Double-Click's hand goes from being stiff to agile in the few minutes after waking never fails to startle Maousse. How is that possible?

***

Double-Click has done enough work on his blog for the morning. As he ends his session, a stream of photos fills the lock screen. He smiles when the group photo taken in Ksar Massa pops up. He looked good with his blond hair and black djellaba.

His name was Ludwig back then.

An encounter changed his life.

3. <u>FALSE LEADS</u>

Double-Click dropped his racket on his last serve – but his gesture did not precede an ecstatic bow before an enthralled French Open audience wildly applauding a hard-won five-set victory over Rafael Nadal. No. He dropped his racket because a sharp bolt of pain shot through his right shoulder.

He had to do something about it this time.

Until then, Double-Click had simply waited for the pain to "go away." But he knew the time had come for him to see a doctor.

He couldn't figure out why the lengthy physiotherapy sessions he had somehow managed to fit into his busy schedule did not alleviate the pain and stiffness in his shoulder.

So, Double-Click went to see all sorts of "specialists." He first consulted Dr. Wang, a Burmese acupuncturist whose office was in the 7th arrondissement of Paris, far from his homeland's dictatorships. The man's needles proved to be as painful as they were ineffective. After that, Double-Click made an appointment with a fluid specialist (cold as ice, but very pretty) who manipulated him to not much avail. He was even introduced to Didi Jen Ghié from The Adventures of Tintin: the Blue Lotus: "It's very simple: I'll cut off your head! Then you will know the truth!" A radical offer which he chose to turn down.

Finally, Double-Click's general practitioner sent him to a neurologist at Saint-Louis Hospital, who failed to detect anything suspicious on the scan. An overjoyed Double-Click was given the all-clear.

But his euphoria was short-lived, as the accumulation of medical clues soon revealed his pathology.

A revelation that came as a shock.

4. <u>THE REVELATION</u>

Double-Click tried posting an ad in the Classifieds:
Looking for a charitable soul willing to deliver bad news
to a happy man from a happy family. A month passed.
No calls, no e-mails, no text messages. Nothing. Not
even a request for information. Who is the usual bearer
of bad news? Most of the time, some sympathetic
stranger (doctor, nurse, police officer) is commissioned
to inform the still-blissfully unaware recipient that the
party's over.

But in Double-Click's case, both diagnosis and
announcement remained almost exclusively within the
family circle. In her capacity as an experienced
practitioner, Double-Click's cardiologist sister Irina
spotted the early signs of a veiled pathology that every
other specialist had failed to see; but she did not feel
emotionally strong enough to share her hypothetical
conclusions with Double-Click himself. In a reassuring
tone, she suggested that he consult her husband Pat,

also a cardiologist at Bichat Hospital. After a few specific questions and a spot of writing, the latter soon aligned his diagnosis with that of his sister.

But, like her, he was in no hurry to hit Double-Click with the bad news without being a hundred percent sure of his appraisal. He recommended his brother-in-law to an eminent neurologist at the Salpêtrière Hospital, who came to the same conclusion as his fellow practitioners and who kept equally quiet about it, preferring to refer Double-Click to yet another confirmatory examination.

Instinct or mere deduction led Double-Click to realize that things were not turning out quite as he had expected. Indeed, if his ailment had been benign, Irina would have reassured him long ago. Still, he was far from imagining that his was the same disease that had made his maternal grandfather's old days a misery, for he thought this condition only affected the elderly.

When the consultation was over, the eminent Salpêtrière neurologist laid a hand on Double-Click's shoulder for what seemed to be a very long time before

seeing him out. This friendly and unusual gesture —
especially from a stranger — was like a foreboding of
things to come.

When Irina called her brother to wish him a happy
birthday in the days that preceded a dreaded
appointment with yet another specialist, his nerves
were frayed from waiting. He told her that all he wanted
for his birthday was "to know the truth."

Well, she couldn't just spill the beans on the phone like
that (and she didn't feel she should anyway, as his
sister), but she asked Pat to call him back the very next
day. Which he did.

After hastily and rather sheepishly wishing him a happy
birthday, Pat took a deep breath... and told Double-Click
that he was suffering from "Parkinson's syndrome.

The news surprised Double-Click more than it worried
him, since he didn't really know what Parkinson's
entailed. Still, something in Pat's voice didn't augur well.
His emotions stifled by his manners and innate modesty,

Double-Click simply thanked Pat for letting him know and put the phone down.

A surge of dizzying anxiety that seemed to stem from a bad dream seized him to the point that he had to make sure he, Double-Click, really was that guy who had just hung the phone up. Yes, there was no doubt about it, he had indeed been the recipient of the call.

He suddenly felt as lonely as an astronaut on a space mission would upon seeing his capsule take off again without him, leaving him stranded in a celestial setting. He hurried back to his study and googled the word "Parkinson's" for the very first time in his life.

As it turns out, the Internet is quite an unsparingly precise source of information on every major disease affecting the human race.

A mere fifteen minutes after entering the word in the world-famous search bar, he had already skimmed through the many blunt descriptions of the disease's symptoms and general evolution. And now, in the silence of his study, Double-Click hears a noise. The familiar sound rises unannounced from the nearby church and fills the country air, echoing around the elegant country house. The bell that rings low and at regular intervals was traditionally known to cast a meditative spell on all living souls. It called for silence as it tolled the death knell.

"They say Parkinson's takes its toll…" he breathes in a desperate attempt to make light of the situation.

But a chill runs down his spine – as if the death bell tolled just for him.

His hopes – a tad ambitious – of everlasting life on earth vanish at that very moment.

He immediately seeks shelter in the nearby Saint-Augustin church. The vast and silent nave seems the best place to put things into perspective and ask the Creator a few questions.

There, he enters into negotiations about his life expectancy on Earth, making sure to add to his prayer that he knows how insignificant his request may sound compared to the promise of eternal life.

His natural anxiety increases tenfold as the reality of the diagnosis dawns on him.

He goes home back to Aure and their four children, who are having dinner. As he tries his best not to let his inner distress show, he realizes how much his family means to him. His heart sinks – soon, he will have to darken their cloudless happiness.

5. <u>FLASHBACK</u>

The dinner is full of joy, as always. All invite Double-Click to sit with them at the round table and join in the fun.

Pretty, elegant and demanding, Aure is also extraordinarily sharp-eyed.

She is as poised as Double-Click is overenthusiastic, as dark-haired as he is blond, as attracted to matter as he is to abstract concepts, and as Pisces as he is Gemini — with all due respect to all the horoscope experts who claim that these two-star signs are anything but compatible. And right now, she is feeding her hungry brood after their day at school or the office.

Anaïs is Aure and Double-Click's eldest daughter. Although she is neither Albanian nor a missionary, her selflessness and joie de vivre earned her the nickname of Sister Teresa. Outgoing, beautiful, funny, cheerful and outspoken (sometimes even cheeky), she masks her anxiety with the odd mood swing that turn her usual saint-like character into a disgruntled grouch.

César is the first son of the aforementioned couple. Nicknamed "Rudy" (for is rude sense of humor) the teenager is sharp and curious, with a witty mind bordering on the caustic. He has inherited Aure's high standards. Although his quest for excellence sometimes drives him to the edge of obsession, it also leads him to make a good – even great – job of everything he undertakes. Reserved by nature, he would at times like to be more of an extrovert.

Antonin is his younger brother. Also good-looking and dark-haired like Aure, he is the outgoing kind: talkative, adaptable, enterprising, and always eager to learn new things – like the guitar and music theory – and make new friends. Antonin would rather spend his time surrounded by nature than by the Paris landscape. Nothing thrills him more than the prospect of a weekend in the countryside.

Max, the youngest, has just entered junior high. Open, bright, funny, and sharp, he draws his energy from his three older siblings. A true competitor at heart, he loves games and can't wait to cross the Champ-de-Mars to play with the "Petits Anges" football team every Wednesday.

Racked by the secret of his diagnosis, Double-Click finds a bittersweet aftertaste to that evening's dinner – as if he were being taken back into everything he has experienced so far with each member of his beloved family.

The highlights of their lives together flash by in a few seconds: he sees his children as babies, smiling, crying, teething, taking their first steps, falling, kindergarten, elementary school, friends, holidays, junior high, kissing, rebelling, clashing, high school, exams, driver's tests... and he feels an irrepressible desire to know what will come next: cigarettes, buddies, dates, beers, first times, preparatory classes, Uni, Grandes Écoles, internships, first jobs...

He recalls their vacations in the mountains and by the sea, the thing that is done in their privileged world.

He remembers when he and Aure were kids, growing up in two magical places in particular: Chéry-sur-Mer, a town that is not coastal despite its name but located somewhere between the N76 road – downgraded to D2076 – and the woods of Sologne; and Rosier-en-Terres, a large Bourbonnais farmhouse nestled in the heart the French countryside.

Chéry-sur-Mer is Aure's hometown. Known as the "Angel of the Sun," her mother whose smile and soft blue eyes enfold you in a halo of kindness still lives there, and her grandchildren still go searching for the place where she keeps her wings at night before going to bed. Her pies and tarts are by far the best in the world. Aure's uncle Gromyko is like a grandfather, only better. His eyes are always sparkling (with champagne more than fizzy water) and although he claims there is nothing to it, he is an incredibly talented magician who can turn any old vegetable patch into a Garden of Eden, any log pile into a wood palace, and even an old Renault 4 EDF into a legendary car. He works harder than anyone I know, always with a smile and a serene attitude.

The jukeboxes and pinball machines are a recent addition to Rosier-en-Terres. Built in 1751, it started out as a noble ensemble of agricultural farms that has since been transformed into a primary residence. Primary, like the warmth exuded by its thick and protective walls and the fond memories built over the years.

Double-Click's children have been as happy as modern kids can be in these two places (days with their cousins or friends, bike rides, theater shows, film shootings, reading, pool games, parties, birthdays, diving in the swimming pool, trips on mopeds, and so on). And Double-Click's childhood was blissful there too, albeit in a more "agricultural" way (feeding pigs, moving cows from one meadow to another, choosing a bull while holding hands with his father – what a memory! – collecting eggs in the henhouse, riding on the tractor, etc.).

Dinner is drawing to an end. Double-Click decides that he won't let anyone or anything, least of all his newfound mortality, rob him of the next episodes of their lives. He wants to stand side by side with Aure and watch their children grow into fulfilled adults.

This, he pledges, will be his war.

6.   <u>SIR JAMES P., AKA OLD HUBERT</u>

In 1817, Sir James Parkinson published a medical paper entitled An Essay on the Shaking Palsy.

Shaking palsy – what a pretty-sounding name for a paradoxical condition whereby paralysis causes agitation.

Six case studies were all it took to prove his point, enough to make today's pharmaceutical giants green with envy as they must call on thousands of volunteers to conduct a clinical trial.

Sixty years after James Parkinson's essay was published, a French neurologist called Jean Martin Charcot brought the London doctor's work into focus and did him the honor of renaming the pathology in question: that's how "Shaking Palsy" became "Parkinson's Disease."

But what has this got to do with Old Hubert? Aure asks Double-Click.

In the post-French Revolution period, while Britain was in political chaos, James Parkinson published nearly twenty political pamphlets. Writing under his own name and his pseudonym "Old Hubert," he called for radical social reforms. In short, he was an activist, without paralysis but with a sharp eye for detail. He is said to have only truly examined one of his patients and to have gathered most of the elements in his study from watching affected pedestrians.

And indeed, Double-Click has noticed that his gait sometimes attracts prying and quite unwelcome glances from other people in the street.

***

Sir James Parkinson had not expected his name to become so famous. And now that it has, does he feel happy about it from beyond the grave? To represent peace like Alfred Nobel does must be quite rewarding, but is there any pride to be derived from embodying a pathology with such negative overtones?

As it turns out – and perhaps this comes as a comfort to him – the name of the very person who prompted James Parkinson's posthumous claim to fame, Jean-Martin Charcot, is associated with an even more serious condition.

Sir James Parkinson, who led a busy life, would probably have preferred to be remembered for his political pamphlets penned under the name Old Hubert and for his active involvement in other causes. In addition to being a doctor, he was a crusader for the rights of abused children and the mentally ill, and more surprisingly still, he was a chemist, a geologist, and a paleontologist.

Unlike his eponymous disease, he was a man worth more than meets the eye.

Sir James P. recently met Jean-Martin Charcot at a doctors' intergenerational meeting up there in Heaven. Although less buoyant than in his youth, the still-lively Sir James P. expressed his dissatisfaction with his name being associated with only one pathology to the detriment of his many other achievements during his spell on Earth. Things got so heated between the two men that a violent magnetic storm broke over the Channel. Their revered dean Hippocrates chipped in to appease the raging debate and called for a more dignified demeanor. Sheepish, the two physicians pledged their obedience to the Greek Father of Medicine and sealed their reconciliation with a hug. Great scientists always find a common ground in the end.

7. <u>**THE ANNOUNCEMENT**</u>

Double-Click kept Old Hubert's revelation to himself for two weeks. His only confidante during this time was his sister Irina, whose soothing support shall be remembered on the Day of Reckoning.   He decides to tell his family about his condition while they are all together spending a weekend in their holiday home in Rosier-en-Terres. He could gently broach the subject upon waking up on Sunday morning, for example, to give everyone some time to come to terms with the news.   Double-Click begins his dreaded announcement in the drowsy warmth of the marital bed. His words cling warily to his throat at first, before taking the plunge and floating the short distance to Aure's ears. Emotion washes over him as he curls up in his beloved wife's arms, and although Aure knows very little about her husband's condition, she intuits from his unwonted abandon that life will never be the same again.   That's it – Old Hubert is now an intimate part of their lives.

And, to be honest, sharing their bed with a stranger had never been on their secret desire list... let alone with an old Englishman, however knighted he may be!

***

Aure had sensed something was up long before the revelation of the diagnosis. Although she couldn't tell precisely what was wrong with her beloved Double-Click, she knew he was different. It was more than mere intuition – her sharp eye had detected the telltale signs.

Now that the truth is out in the open, Aure has no intention of hiding it. She had to keep a secret as a child and it took her a long time to get over it. She now wants to avoid a repeat experience at all costs. She grew up without a father and it was nearly forty years before she could talk about it. He wasn't dead, he even had a long life; he simply chose not to disclose an extramarital affair. Was it to spare his lawful wife the unnecessary grief? Probably. Besides, is lying by omission really a lie? After all, she never asked any questions.   Aure's extraordinarily kind mother, whom the grandchildren have renamed "Angel of the Sun," made up for her absent father. And although she raised Aure by herself, she did a better job than most mother-and-father couples. Aure is now proud of her unusual upbringing, but back then she mostly felt different from the other kids – and this weighed heavily on her heart. Aure met Double-Click for the first time during a night out with friends. She was instantly drawn by his kindness and thoughtfulness. She even found him funny. He did not seem to mind about her family situation; in fact, it looked like he wanted to repair the damage caused by the Absent One, but it ran much deeper than he thought – the roots of her angst had fossilized. It took him seven years to propose to her. She went through moments of doubt, to the point of wondering if he really was as unaffected by social conventions as he had claimed. A diffuse sense of guilt dampened her usual active and energetic self for a while. Despite being a talented artist, she had no desire to emancipate herself through work. She wanted a big family, not to make her mother's dream come true but because she knew it would make her happy.   Double-Click's encounter with Old Hubert was like a bad reenactment of the past. She had just gotten rid of her father's ghost, and now the man of her life whom she saw as invincible was threatened by an unexpected illness. Her initial dismay was soon eclipsed by other concerns as she realized that their lives were about to be upended.

* * *

Double-Click remembers when he and Aure sat with their elder children Anaïs and Rudy in the living room on Avenue Émile Pouvillon to break the news to them that life isn't always as rosy as their mother's lipstick. They tried their best to keep their emotions in check, and chose their words carefully to sound reassuring, Anaïs and César perceived their underlying fear in the face of a mysterious but very real disease.   Raising children is a humbling task, Double-Click told himself as he realized that trying to conceal his own anxiety to reassure his two teenagers was having the opposite effect.   The news shook them up of course, as it did Antonin and Max when they were later let into the secret. They, too, have since learned to put on a brave face, but their direct questions and unconscious remarks betray concerns that Double-Click wishes he could have spared them. He guesses the silent apprehension behind their joyful attitudes and increasingly sharp jokes. They certainly know how to surf the Net, and Hadopi does not monitor the flurry of shameless patients making crude confessions on multifarious medical sites. They must have found the news of their dad's illness quite daunting indeed...   They preferred the good old, normal version of their Double-Clout – as they had facetiously nicknamed him even though he never laid as much as a finger on them. They wished they could turn the clock back to when things weren't so bad after all. And what if their father's condition was hereditary?

***

César and Anaïs had a chat together after Double-Click and their mother broke the news to them in their favorite room. The white marble fireplace will remain etched in their memory, along with the blond parquet floor, the triple oval-shaped concentric moldings, and the six large and clear windows offering a view of the 113 meter-long avenue Barbey d'Aurevilly whose buildings overlook the Eiffel Tower. Similar in style yet all unique, the magnificent cut-stone edifices echo their own stately residence at 2 avenue Émile Pouvillon, even more majestic in their eyes. The forever kingdom of their childhood.   They had been exemplary overlords, lavishly entertaining their friends, celebrating Christmases, christenings and communions, opening the ball under the benevolent-yet-watchful eye of Aure, the beloved mistress of all their ceremonies. They shared so many happy times as a family and with their friends that their laughter and giggles put a smile on the walls. Double-Click's desk stands with its back to an upright piano in a corner of the living room. They often wonder why he spends so much time on his computer. Is it for his job as a consultant? And anyway, as their friends always ask, "What is a consultant?"   They wonder about that strange day when their role as the elders was reinstated, after being temporarily jeopardized by their fast-growing-up younger siblings Antonin and Max. They could tell Double-Click's announcement was important from his solemn tone of voice. He had seemed absorbed in his thoughts and had barely smiled when,

after hearing of Old Hubert's arrival, César tried to lighten the unusually solemn atmosphere with a joke along the lines of "we won't let you cut the pizzas anymore if you start shaking too much!" Shaking – the emblematic symbol of his pathology. After announcing his illness to his two older children, Double-Click walked Anaïs back to her studio on l'avenue de Suffren where she had recently moved in above her grandmother Odette's apartment.

Independence is all well and good, but living alone can be tough sometimes! Her friends have all moved on and taken different higher education routes according to their aspirations. They still see each other from time to time, but the days when they used to meet up at the

school gates every morning were well and truly over...
It's hard to be alone, looking up Old Hubert on the
Internet. It all seems so unfair. Old Hubert has nothing
to do with Double-Click. They have nothing in common,
nothing to share – the Englishman knocked at the wrong
door. Her father doesn't belong to that Hubert guy, he
has no right over him. He is her Double-Click, the one
who used to accompany her to school, help her with her
math homework, tease her – the one who loves her like
a father loves his daughter.   She is also thinking about
her upcoming 20th birthday. She'd like to have a big
party with all her friends, and she hopes that handsome
DJ who was at her cousin Cam's party will come too.
Sure, he had a Pokémon name, Chikorita – but it doesn't
really matter when your own father is called Double-
Click.

Strong-willed and pragmatic as always, Anaïs finds a lot
of comfort in the words of Slim, Double-Click's new
physiotherapist.

8. <u>SLIM</u>

The submarine sonar humming from deep inside Slim's pants pocket is emitted by his phone, an accessory as essential as his BMW C1 on which he races from one patient to the next without the burden of a helmet. Slim brings the device to his ear with his left hand without letting go of his bedridden patient's leg: "Hello, could I speak to Slim, please? I am calling on the recommendation of Dr. Z." (Silence)   Slim is perplexed – he swore he wouldn't take any new patients.   And yet, a week later, Slim finds himself parking his scooter outside a beautiful Haussmannian building at the corner of avenues Bourdonnais and Émile Pouvillon. He goes up to the third floor and is ushered into an oval-shaped living room with windows overlooking the Champ-de-Mars to the south and a jammed intersection to the northeast. Double-Click looks really young, and his wife looks even younger.   After brief introductions, he tries to reassure them a little by explaining that the pathology does not significantly reduce life expectancy and that regular stretching helps maintain muscle flexibility – not to mention, as with any disease, the benefits of a positive attitude.   As it always happens when patients are still reeling from the shock of their diagnosis, Slim struggles through the first sessions. He tries to reassure Double-Click and answer his anxious questions about the evolution of his pathology as best he can while looking out for any symptoms that may help in pinpointing his patient's condition, as some forms of it evolve more quickly than others. But he chooses not to share this information with Double-Click just yet.   It took a few months for Double-Click's initial shock to subside, during which time he learned to identify and tame the – then – mild manifestations of the disease. But he still feels like he is journeying with a stranger, a transient passenger. He can't get used to the idea that he is suffering from a chronic disease, in other words, one that is incurable – three seemingly harmless syllables whose significance becomes striking to whomever is thus affected.

***

Slim rings the bell, and the door opens. As usual, he lays his coat on the entrance bench and shows Double-Click some pictures on his phone. It has become a ritual between them.   Slim is a handsome man who forms a lovely couple with his sweet and charming Celia. They have just given birth to an adorable and energetic Giuletta, a beautiful baby loved and cherished by her parents judging by the number of pics on Slim's phone.

 Slim is now very much a part of Double-Click's life, ever since Dr. Z asked him to turn Double-Click into a contortionist to claim the sought-after title of "Elastic Man" in reference to the most flexible woman in the world, "Elastic Woman," better known as "Zlata."   Let's be honest, it seems impossible to surpass the unsurpassable Zlata; still, Double-Click clings to this goal because it's worth it, as Slim explained at a recent conference: "Most patients have difficulty initiating movements, especially those requiring precision and semi-automatic gestures such as walking or writing."

Slim added that patients with this condition must absolutely remain active if they want to maintain their quality of life – and his words stayed with Double-Click.

All set for flexibility. As for slowness, Double-Click won't ask an already snowed-under Slim; he shall call on the great Arturo Brachetti instead. Indeed – and although he hopes it will never come to it – buttoning his shirt in the morning takes him so long, and longer every time, that he might one day end up fastening the last button at bedtime.

****

Slim and Double-Click meet once or twice a week. As they get to know each other better, they realize that they share the same sense of humor and have many interests in common. Slim is happy to visit Double-Click and vice-versa, but the physiotherapist never loses sight of his initial therapeutic mission.   At a conference, Slim displays a series of photos showing Double-Click struggling to perform various flexibility exercises, his face covered by a Smiley to preserve his anonymity. As he returns to his seat in the audience, he is congratulated by the young woman sitting next to him. They get talking. She works at the Hospital Salpêtrière.

9. <u>MONA</u>

A month after the diagnosis, Double-Click contacted a specialist in "motivational disorders" who goes by the name of Mona. Coined at a time when the word "suffering" was persona non grata, the term was trending in psychiatric circles to indicate depressive tendencies. Feeling quite uneasy but knowing he had to open up, he first quoted Steve Jobs: "Sometimes life's going to hit you in the head with a brick." She nodded without saying a word. Her job is precisely to speak with those who got hit in the head with a brick – or worse. Enough to compel some to wall up.   She takes few notes but Double-Click invariably feels she is listening attentively, whether he talks about his travels, his concerns for his children, his mother, his marriage, his job.   She is an accomplished practitioner who knows exactly when Double-Click tries to sidestep the harsh and unsightly reality, the insidiously unsettling truth.   A therapy well worth a little poem.

My birthday was yesterday.   Today is another day…
The day they name my oppressor,   Like a time-warp
usurper…   An old folks' condition affecting the younger
   To get back at junior for targeting senior?   Spiteful
hospital…   My kingdom for a shrink.   Turns out it's a
she-shrink.   I speak, I unravel!   She listens as if I were
a marvel.   Her smile is the pill.

****

Mona loves her job. She finds the human psyche
fascinating and considers soul and spirit as one.   She
has been Double-Click's therapist for a few years now.
He comes to see her as his mood fancies. Mona recalls
their first session.   He was one of her first patients,
after she graduated. She felt a little intimidated, but he
was far too troubled to notice. He quoted Steve Jobs as
if to make it easier on her. He had just found out about
his disease, and the diagnosis had upended his outlook –
overnight. He who was usually so confident, so proud of
his success, saw what he had taken for an invincible

protective armor pop like a soap bubble. He poured out all his fears, natural daughters born of his forced union with his disease. They had grown, hidden away, feeding on dark thoughts that Double-Click could no longer dispel. Mona was used to it. She pacified him while helping him face his fears.   The sessions succeeded one another. He learned to overcome his reserve and open up. He often walks into her office with a calm demeanor, pretending all is fine. But she senses something is not quite right, and a few minutes later, his words no longer hide his trouble. Confiding brings comfort. Only a few stubborn thoughts won't come out – they are simply too painful. The magic of his earnest self-mockery keeps them at bay.   Sometimes she doesn't hear from him for weeks. It probably means that he's fine, but you never know… He could at least have the courtesy to spare her the concern.

10. <u>ZORRO</u>

Double-Click has an appointment with Dr. Z, his neurologist since he was first diagnosed. The practitioner has extensive dosage knowledge and is well-versed in the art of mixing drugs. "Balancing" a patient's treatment – as they say in the trade – requires as much finesse as it does to shake a Caipirinha capable of washing away your sorrows without getting you drunk. Dr. Z is a medical authority. In addition to caring for his patients, he is concerned about the challenges encountered by their loved ones when dealing with a condition like Double-Click's. And rightly so. Dr. Z is right to care about the family circle – meaning the collateral victims of the patient, those whose mission is to grin and bear it.

They don't complain, but everybody needs a little TLC from time to time. Thus, "caring for the caregivers" has become Dr. Z's motto. But let's think of them as the "loved ones," no need to give in to excessive pathos with words like "caregivers," as if one were on death row.

***

Dr. Z has made up his mind this time: he will retire in one or two years at the most. He has been talking about his impending retirement for months, but he finds it hard to give up his calling, and his patients finally managed to convince him that there's no need to rush into anything. Still, he'll have to set a date someday.

Curious to know how many patients he treated in his long career, Dr. Z turns to the Internet – easier than counting. There was the case, blown out of proportion, of a French physician who saw 91 patients in one day. That times 200, i.e. the number of days in a year, means he would clock up 720,000 consultations over 40 years.

An American practitioner who asked himself this question before Dr. Z went through appointment diaries over periods of fifteen to twenty years. He came to the likely figure of forty thousand patients throughout the career of a well-established physician.

Slightly unsettled by the high numbers, Dr. Z lowers his own patient-count to somewhere between fifteen and twenty thousand as his specialty requires longer-than-average consultations.

If Double-Click knew of these figures, he might be more lenient whenever Dr. Z repeats the same questions from one appointment to the next. No doctor can retain every detail of their patients' lives. On the other hand, no patient can imagine being just one among many others. And yet...

Dr. Z walks Aure and Double-Click to the door. The latter appreciates his practitioner's dry sense of humor. Once, in late spring, he told Dr. Z that he wanted to swim a lot to stay in shape. To which the doctor replied that two of his patients who were suffering from the same disease had drowned the previous summer.

***

Since then, Double-Click only ever swims where his feet can touch the bottom, and always within eyeshot of his family.

Dr. Z's specialty is indeed special: it entails warning patients about the risks of certain physical symptoms, but without worrying them so much that it crushes their high spirits. And as it turns out, Dr. Z is very good at getting that type of message across, with a calm voice and just a hint of wit.

***

Tired after his consultation with Dr. Z, Double-Click kills time surfing the Internet while waiting for bedtime. He comes across a video by the INA: the first episode of The Shadoks. He bursts out laughing.

"It hasn't aged at all!"

He wistfully recalls his childhood when he would sit with his parents and sisters every night in front of the TV to watch an episode, too short as always.

The Shadoks had mottos that seem to have been specially devised for Double-Click and his fellow sufferers.

Waking up: "I get tired of sleeping!"

With Slim, his physiotherapist: "If it hurts, it's good for you!"

Researchers could also do with: "If there's no solution, there's no problem."

And if Double-Click's condition takes a turn for the worse: "Sorry, I forgot I had amnesia."

11. <u>WHY?</u>

Once the shock subsided, Double-Click asked the question everyone asks upon discovering they have a pathology that nothing seemed to predispose them to: WHY ME?

Double-Click searched the Web for statistics that would shed some light on why Old Hubert took a liking to him. Amid the maze of scientific and medical sites, he came across a blog written in true American fashion: well-documented and structured, up to date – and an award-winner. Its author describes the type of person most likely to suffer from Parkinson's: Male, with blond hair. One of his ancestors got it... "Wait!" Double-Click exclaims, "this reminds me of something. Why not look at it the other way around? Let me describe the person least likely to be a victim of Old Hubert." The anti-victim is a woman under 60, "non-Caucasian" (meaning anything but white-skinned), with brown hair and without a history of the disease among her parents. She is neither Amish nor a farmer. She never had head trauma, nor did she work in a manganese mine. She doesn't do drugs. She is not a doctor, dentist, teacher, lawyer, scientist, computer programmer, or gamekeeper. She works in the fields of production or transport, but she is not a welder. She smokes and drinks coffee. If she's American, she doesn't live in Nebraska.   That's all well and good, but... what conclusions is Double-Click supposed to draw from this? Not many, he muses while considering some very personal issues: "Aure, can you cancel our trip to Nebraska. We don't really need to go see the rednecks after all, do we? Oh, and I'm not sure I want to visit the Amish country with our cousins from Philadelphia, I don't feel like watching backward people dressed in black wash their laundry by hand."   "Now that's a good use of statistics," he concludes, although not quite convinced. "In any case, a blog is a great idea! I'm going to write one too. I'm up early in the mornings, I should find the time. I wonder what San Antonio will think of that.

***

San Antonio is due to visit the Double-Clicks that weekend. Everyone is looking forward to it. San Antonio is Double-Click's second cousin. Maybe they met when they were kids, but they don't remember. They first got to know each other when San Antonio's uncle, abbot and bishop of a Swiss abbey, invited them to prepare Aure and Double-Click's marriage with his soon-to-be ordained nephew.   San Antonio had accepted the responsibility. It was his first marriage. There's a first time for everything. To preserve his modesty and out of respect for his office, San Antonio had let Double-Click introduce him: "Bright, handsome, funny sometimes, and a true man of faith." Aure had nodded in silence. She who had expected her marriage preparation to be led by an imposing bishop in an austere church found herself chatting with a good-looking and courteous man the same age as them, in the middle of a verdant meadow in Switzerland – as if immersed in her favorite series when she was a teenager: The Thorn Birds.   Aure had been so hanging on the cleric's every word that Double-Click thought she might become a nun instead of marrying him. Fortunately, there was no convent in the abbey. San Antonio went on to play a recurrent part in the lives of the Double-Clicks, from christenings to first communions and confirmations, and all times four. Their initial wedding ceremony had become a reference. When Max's confirmation marked the last of the children's sacraments, it didn't put an end to San Antonio's regular trips to Paris, where he had once lived as a student and which he loves. And whenever he visits, Aure always goes out to her way to make him feel welcome. The Double Clicks find San Antonio's wit very uplifting. He started visiting more often when Double-Click got the bad news. He found the right words and texts to help Double-Click and Aure through their initial bewilderment. San Antonio became their confidant over time. They find his wise words soothing and appreciate his insights.   Naturally, San Antonio encourages Double-Click to create his blog – that's all the latter needed to get started.

***

"What should I call it?" wonders Double-Click. "The Shakedown on Parkinson's? The play on words is a bit grim. Parkin-Son of A...? Nah, my education won't allow me. Let's go for Son of P...arkin, I like the sound of it, and who knows I might even get an award for it!"   To start his blog, Double-Click searches the Web for more information on his condition. He first focuses on the disease's general mechanisms.   Enthusiastic, Double-Click uploads his first post and decides to personify Parkinson's disease as Old Hubert. Double-Click is pleased to present Son of P...arkin, the first blog dedicated to your most important asset, the black substance – the brain of your brain!

***

Son of P...arkin, the Mind-boggling Blog:

Who Am I?

I am at the heart of the nervous system, I integrate information, control movement and ensure cognitive functions.   I am the most protected organ in the body. I weigh about 1.3 kg. I am bathed in cerebrospinal fluid (CSF). My meninges refer to the three layers of protective tissue that cover me. I am made up of two cerebral hemispheres, the right and the left, united by the corpus callosum (network of fibers), and the cerebellum, a kind of "little brain" located in the lower area of the brain that controls balance.   My main nutrient is glucose. I am highly vascularized and therefore highly oxygenated. My cerebral hemisphere is formed by the frontal lobe, associated with reasoning, language functions, and voluntary motor coordination; the parietal lobe, associated with consciousness of the body and its surroundings; the occipital lobe, involved in the integration of messages; and the temporal lobe that controls hearing, memory, and emotions.   I also have four cerebral ventricles, cavities where the cerebrospinal fluid circulates. Lastly, my central grey nuclei are in the middle of all this. Also known as basal ganglia, they are associated with behavior control and learning.   I am Double-Click's brain.   I must tell you that Old Hubert probably started tampering with my cognitive functions some fifteen years ago. I fought against him for a long time without Double-Click noticing

– until it became impossible for me to make up for all the damage he had caused. Ideally, he should have been eradicated the moment he showed his ugly head, but his intrusion was undetectable.

***

Going over his first post, Double-Click looks perplexed: it almost entirely plagiarizes a scientific website. To ease his guilt a little, he tells himself that his blog is there to inform his brothers and sisters in pathology. He had to set the scene first.   Son of P...arkin's first five visitors identified by Google Analytics congratulate Double-Click: they are called Aure, Anaïs, César, Antonin, and Max. Being a prophet in one's own country sounds like a good start.

Okay then, write a book
about your disease
if that's what you want
but please,
make it less of a drag!
GABS.

12. <u>THE BLOG</u>

The following week, Double-Click decides to pull out all the stops with his blog by addressing four main themes:

- The symptoms, as they are multiple and unknown to most people – including Double-Click's family and friends,

– His own cures to fight Old Hubert,

– Preconceived ideas: everyone is scared by Old Hubert! You, your loved ones, and everybody else,

– Research, as one can't find the strength to fight the disease without hope for a discovery that will relieve symptoms.

To launch his blog, Double-Click thinks that a drawing will speak louder than long speeches. He recently came across a sketch that depicted one of his condition's little-known symptoms.

Son of P...arkin, the Mind-boggling Blog

Poker Face

Double-Click's condition does have positive sides, but to fully appreciate them one must be particularly fond of exploring caves.

Take card games, for example. Double-Click, who keeps losing at War, turns out to be an excellent poker player.

Although less talented than poker legend Daniel Negreanu who has won in excess of $35 million so far, and in addition to his own innate skill, Double-Click benefits from one of his disease's little-known effects.

According to vulgaris-medical.com: 'For a movement to be fluid, an agonist muscle must contract at the same time as an antagonist muscle relaxes or lengthens. This synchronicity is hard to achieve for Parkinson's disease sufferers. It shows in their faces, impassive, expressionless, with eyelids that rarely blink.'

Sounds sexy, mumbles Double-Click; still, there's some consolation to be found in his newfound poker bluffing skills.

Moreover, given the rate at which Double-Click's face freezes, the aforementioned Daniel might need to start shaking in his boots. And it feels like sweet revenge to make someone else shake.

Decoding the Parkinsonian face

(And why you should care)

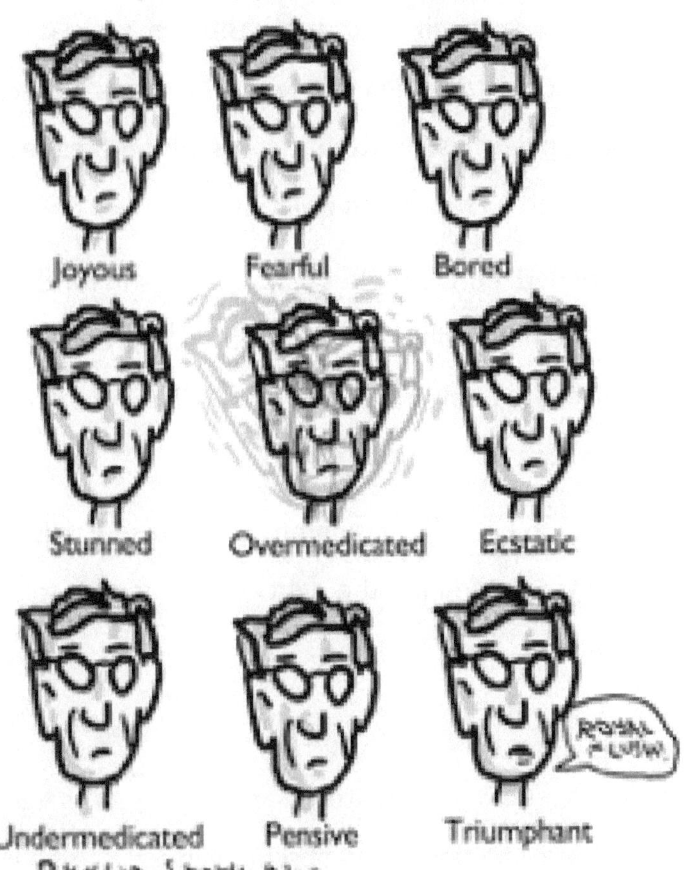

***

Peter Dunlap-Shohl is smiling: his latest book turned out just as he hoped it would. Entitled My Degeneration, a Journey Through Parkinson's, the humorous graphic novel depicts his dealings with Old Hubert. A Facebook pop-up catches his attention: it's a friend request from a stranger, a Frenchman called Double-Click.

Intrigued, Peter inquires as to the reason for this request via the messaging service. Double-Click replies that he is looking to publish one of his drawings, Pokerface, in his own blog on Old Hubert.

Proud to hear that his name travelled overseas, Peter grants Double-Click the rights to his drawing for a few dollars.

***

Double-Click immediately warmed to Peter's humble self-introduction as 'an obscure cartoonist who lives far, far away.'

Given the 7,528 km between them, they only communicate by email. The time difference is so big that one's bedtime is the other's wake-up call – whenever they actually manage to catch some sleep!

That reminds Double-Click of a team of Swiss researchers and their strange discovery about sleep. He must tell Peter to check it out on his blog, 'Son of P...arkin'.

13. <u>VIRTUOUS CIRCLE</u>

Remember The Invaders, that TV series from the 1970s with David Vincent in the lead role?

The opening narration was fantastic: '... For him, it began one lost night on a lonely country road, looking for a shortcut that he never found...'

***

Son of P...arkin, the Mind-boggling Blog

<u>Sleep</u>

Double-Click's sleep is like David Vincent's shortcut: never to be found again. Like the Shadoks, he is forced to come to the conclusion that "sleeping makes him tired."

He could even add: "The less I sleep, the more I am affected and the more I am affected, the less I sleep and the more I am affected..."

A Swiss researcher at the University of Geneva has established a bidirectional link between Parkinson's disease and sleep.

'Patients suffering from Parkinson's disease show an inverse correlation between deep sleep, also called slow-wave sleep, and the severity of symptoms.'

In other words: the more you sleep, the less tired you are, the better you feel, and the easier you walk.

'In describing the observed association as very robust, the researcher suggested that improving the quality of the deep sleep phase could prove therapeutic in Parkinson's disease.'

WOW! thought Double-Click. So, a good night's sleep could help alleviate the symptoms... only trouble is, it's the very symptoms that keep him awake.

Although he was never much of a heavy sleeper, he used to have the occasional lie-in and wake up full of energy for the day. But now, the short nights that end at four or five in the morning sometimes morph into long naps until that time when others go to bed.

And instead of waking up fully rested and ready to start the day, he is stirred from slumber by a cramp, the inability to turn, or an urge to pee. Nothing truly alarming – more like a discomfort.

'If this bidirectional relationship is proven, sleep disorders could be part of a vicious circle that accelerates the neurodegenerative process. Consequently, improved sleep quality could slow the progression of the disease.'

But of course! Double-Click glimpses a glimmer of hope – healing is possible!

All he needs to do is reverse the trend: The more I sleep, the less I am affected, and the less I am affected, the more I sleep and the less I am affected...

How come he never thought of it before? The Swiss nailed it. It's a real Copernican revolution – except that it says nothing about how to actually get a good night's sleep.

***

Slim, too, has been feeling quite sleep-deprived lately. Baby Giuletta's arrival is a blessing that changed his life – including his nights.

He often sleeps even less than his own patients… one of whom, Double-Click, seems different, as if he were elsewhere. Maybe Slim should have a word with Mona about it. Sure, they're bound by professional secrecy, but it would be for the patient's good.

***

As for Double-Click himself, he feels fine – apart from the fact that he no longer feels anything.

14. <u>SENS INTERDITS</u>

Not all of Double-Click's symptoms are motor-related. Some, more pernicious, affect his senses, as if they were not longer accessible... as if they were forbidden... 'Sens interdits'...

Son of P...arkin, the Mind-boggling Blog

<u>Smell</u>

Let's begin with the sense of smell and observe the natural order of things: the more Double-Click's body gives off the distinctive odor associated with Parkinson's, the less he can detect it. This is the paradoxical conclusion of two independent discoveries.

The first one was led by a Scottish woman nicknamed 'Supernose', who could just as well hail from Bergerac like playwright Edmond Rostand's famously large-nosed Cyrano!

'Researchers will study the possibility of diagnosing Parkinson's disease from body odors, based on the testimony of a woman whose 'super sense of smell' detected the degenerative disease's telltale scent on her husband.'

'Supernose' told her story to journalists from all over the world.

"It was a sort of a musky odor. My husband worked as an anesthetist, and since the operating room can get really stuffy, I thought maybe he was just sweating more."

As for neurologists, at least those with a 'nose', Double-Click pictures them sniffing their patients during the first examination while their spouses look on in bewilderment.

The second discovery was that the telltale smell could not be detected by the sufferers themselves.

70 to 90% of Parkinson's disease patients may have a reduced sense of smell!

The disease crawls beneath one's skin a little more with each passing day... and perhaps all the way up to the nose, who knows?

The journalist from Pif isn't happy about having to do the interview. Just because you run a magazine called Pif doesn't mean you should send your reporters on every single trail about smell. Then again, he and his editor never got on – that probably explains why he was picked to cover this particularly tricky topic.

What could he possibly say to interest the weekly magazine's readers, aged 7 to 15? He's totally stuck for inspiration.

First of all, he's not particularly fond of the subject. Plus, he didn't take to that woman, the one who can sniff out Old Hubert like a bloodhound. She looked at him as if she wanted to bore a hole in his soul. Sure, he is quite a handsome man, but there was not a hint of seduction in her gaze. What he saw in her eyes was a form of concern, compassion even.

That was odd, he reflects as he settles into seat 7A after boarding the airbus. He gazes out the round window at Scotland's receding coastline. Time for a nap. He falls asleep. His plane is approaching Charles de Gaulle airport by the time he wakes up, clear-headed. The nap did him good. He grimaces as he reaches for his carry-on luggage in the overhead bin. It's that nagging pain in his shoulder again! But the pain is soon gone – his face relaxes.

***

Double-Click is thrilled. 'Supernose' brought him luck: his post attracted fifty visitors in the last three days, including one from the USA and one from Morocco – not to mention the two 'likes' and the three 'shares'.

Enough to put him in high spirits for the whole day.

15. <u>INCONGRUOUS REMEDIES</u>

First, there were the symptoms. Now is the time for remedies and hope. Searching the web for inspiration, Double-Click is struck by the amount of discoveries of all kinds made by researchers around the world.

***

Son of P...arkin, the Mind-boggling Blog

<u>Tango, Chocolate, Coffee...</u>

Double-Click has taken up new habits, such as tango. According to neurologists from McGill University in Canada, it's 'a great way to fight Parkinson's disease.'

He has also taken to eating tons of dark chocolate since researchers from the Dresden University of Technology in Germany found that chocolate also helps to slow the progression of the disease. This conclusion was reached after 23 patients were given 50 grams of chocolate twice daily for one week. Some consumed white chocolate, containing 0% cocoa, while the others were given dark chocolate with at least 85% cocoa content. The following week, the patients who had consumed white chocolate were given dark chocolate, and vice versa.

The protocol thus devised by the German researchers sounds like a dream. They spent weeks choosing the best medicine among all kinds of delicious chocolates: white, dark, milk? With or without hazelnuts? 70%, 77% or 85% cocoa content? Beans from Java or Peru? 200 grams in one take or in several, throughout the day? So many scientific questions!

In addition to chocolate, Double-Click also started drinking a lot more coffee as researchers discovered that it can reduce motor symptoms such as slowness of movement, stiffness, tremors, and balance disorders.

As for wine, he no longer drinks it; rather, he sips it. Indeed, according to Dr. Stephen Taylor of the University of Queensland, when absorbed slowly the resveratrol in red wine appears to alleviate symptoms. But Double-Click, who for the past three days has been holding in his mouth a swig of Saint-Pourçain red produced in Chareil-

Cintrat by Michel and Catherine Bonne-Terre without noticing any positive effect on his symptoms, wonders what 'absorbed slowly' really means.

Double-Click has tried every diet out there, and they all work! Especially the glass of red with a big chunk of dark chocolate. But, to be honest, it works for everything – and everyone.

***

Talking about these incongruous remedies with Aure, he confesses his disappointment with the results. She suggests that he turns to Chinese medicine instead.

16. <u>THE GV-SPOT</u>

With Dr. Wang, Double-Click learned that stimulating the GV spot, or point, is the best way to fight the symptoms forged by Old Hubert. Of course, Double-Click can't wait to share the astounding news on his blog.

***

Son of P...arkin, the Mind-boggling Blog

<u>Is the Ear an Erogenous Zone?</u>

Hang on... the GV spot is located somewhere on the crown of the head. Although the pun is funny, it has nothing to do whatsoever with the female G-spot, named after the gynecologist Ernst Gräfenberg. Now, he was a smart guy! According to Wikipedia, however, there is no consensus in the scientific community on the actual existence of the G-spot.

As for the GV spot, Double-Click found the following self-massage guide online on Ooreka:

'The most important acupuncture point for treating Parkinson's disease is named GV 20. Located at the top of the head, about 6 to 7 cm above the posterior hairline and halfway between the top of the ears, it is the twentieth point of the governor vessel meridian. Pay particular attention to the areas above the ears, the temples (in front of the upper third of the ears) and the upper part of the skull (parietal bones). Also massage the ears.'

Double-Click admits to having indulged in the above-described cranial onanism. But it didn't do much, except give him bright red ears and a dose of embarrassment when Aure enquired about their crimson color.

The massages would probably be more efficient with a little help from another person. But volunteers are thin on the grounds of the 7th-arrondissement, and even Double-Click's trusted physiotherapist, Slim, has refused to lend a hand.

The post on unknown remedies was such a resounding success that the Dresden University of Technology officially asked Double-Click to publish an erratum, to restore the honor of the researchers who showed the benefits of chocolate on Parkinson's disease. Double-Click reluctantly complied to the request.

Erratum:

Double-Click apologizes for his jokes about the curative powers of chocolate, and for any damage he may have caused to the reputation of excellence of Dresden University of Technology.

***

Double-Click is rather upset about the consequences of his erratum: readers have unsubscribed from his blog and left harsh comments on his lack of seriousness and conviction.

He is trying to figure out the best response when he suddenly remembers something: he has an appointment with a job candidate at 5 p.m. at his Haussmann Boulevard office. He rushes out to the Solférino metro station. Today is June 24th – what a coincidence! It's a bright and sunny day out, with a temperature averaging

25 degrees Celsius. Lovely!

17. <u>THE CANDIDATES</u>

As he enters the offices of the consulting firm he co-founded, Double-Click fondly recalls the great entrepreneurial success he shared with his long-time partners and friends, Johnny Guitar (who encouraged him to go for it) and Steve Short (who stuck with him when others pulled out). He is in a great mood.

His partners are rather benevolent towards him. They trust his experience and judgment (or at least they pretend they do). So, among other tasks, Double-Click takes great pleasure in conducting interviews. They are like all-important moments of truth where the candidate's true character is revealed. And when the latter turns out to be brilliant, a game of seduction sets in that can get quite thrilling – especially when the candidate is a bright, educated, and funny blue-eyed brunette with slightly loose hair.

But what do the candidates think of Double-Click when he greets them at reception? The one he met this morning must have thought: He doesn't look very friendly. It's going to be tough. So much for the poker-face effect.

And Double-Click's restless night probably got him thinking: He is walking in a funny way. Maybe he hurt himself playing football or rugby – but he's not built for that kind of sport.

During an interview Double-Click conducted the week before, he noticed that the candidate seemed perplexed while watching him take notes. Perhaps she was wondering: Why are the letters so small, maybe he doesn't want me to read what he is writing, it's not a good sign. Her apparent confusion troubled Double-Click to the point that his voice became weaker and less clear. He imagined her thinking, What's the matter with him, can't he articulate and speak louder? This thought troubled him even more, and to top it all, he started trembling! At a loss, as the interview was drawing to an end, he said: "It's cold in here, don't you think? The air conditioning needs fixing!" The candidate remained silent; she wasn't sure what to make of it: it was June 24th, and the office was quite hot from the sun-drenched windows. Was he being funny, or was he deranged?

***

Candide A. was pleased with her interview with Double-Click. After seven years working for a leading American consulting firm where she cut her teeth as a consultant and then as a manager in financial services, she was looking for a change.

Thus, when a headhunter retained by Double-Click's firm approached her, she thought Why not give it a go?

She was waiting in the reception area when Double-Click appeared. He was on time. He greeted her with a warm smile and asked her to follow him. She loved his genuine smile and honest handshake. When they reached the interview room, he went through her resume. Had he read it before?

He put her at ease and introduced himself in a casual
way. Then, unsurprisingly, he asked her about her
background and motivation. His questions were precise,
and she answered them with ease.

She noticed that he was taking scrawly, quasi-illegible
notes. She tried to decipher them, in vain. Perhaps he
did not want her to know what he was writing. He asked
her more questions, but in a much lower voice. She was
struggling to understand what he was saying, but she
didn't dare ask him to repeat. So, she winged it by
adroitly eluding the subject and pulling a charming face.
It worked better than she thought: his right hand started
to shake. When Double-Click saw her to the door, he
told her she would soon hear from them about a
potential second interview.

They parted company. Later, while waiting for her train
at métro Glacière, she remembered Double-Click's
remark about the air conditioning – she must have
troubled him. This thought made her smile: Things are
off to a good start!

18. <u>DUCHOVNY VS. DERRICK</u>

"Right, enough about the candidate. I'd like to get back to my symptoms. Actually, there's one in particular I'm a bit shy to mention," says a blushing Double-Click.

***

Son of P...arkin, the Mind-boggling Blog

<u>Kama Sutra</u>

The Kama Sutra is an ancient Hindu text dating back to the early centuries of our era. And although its name alone arouses curiosity, the pornographic revolution (yes, he dares to say it) introduced by the Internet has turned the Kama Sutra into the sexual-fantasy version of the Lascaux Caves compared to Duane Hanson's hyper-realistic Supermarket Lady.

But what has any of this got to do with Double-Click who, as far as one knows, has never practiced the Kama Sutra? Well, let's consider it a preamble to the fact that his libido goes up and down according to the whims of his pathology.

The lowdown:

'The analysis of sexual function in 75 Parkinson's sufferers (32 female, 43 male) indicates a loss of libido (47%), troubles in reaching orgasm (75%), and sexual dissatisfaction (37.5%) among female Parkinson's sufferers.'

Double-Click can't help smiling at the thought of researchers exploring their patients' "sexual functioning" after having thoroughly sniffed them during diagnosis.

The rise of sap:

'Alternatively, all dopamine treatments are thought to improve one's sex drive by fueling sexual desire. This is a rare complication that only affects young patients.'

Needless to say, the above-mentioned libido fluctuations don't do much for Double-Click's sexual fulfilment: his sex drive can be compared to David

Duchovny's in Californication (Season 1) one day, and the next, to Detective Derrick's in the eponymous series (Season 25).

Double-Click is happy he managed to say a few words about libido in his blog. He has overcome his natural shyness and feels in great form thanks to his dernier cri anticyclonic system.

19. **ANTICYCLONE**

Before Old Hubert, Double-Click was an optimistic and cheerful guy who couldn't figure out why some of his friends felt depressed at times.

***

Son of P...arkin, the Mind-boggling Blog

<u>Anti-procrastination</u>

Isn't life just great? A nice job, a darling of a wife, gorgeous, funny, and smart kids, loving sisters, parents still young-at-heart, financial security, close friends...

And then... two to three years before he was diagnosed with Parkinson's, his family and friends thought he had changed, he was less fun, more boring, and he didn't even want to celebrate his forthcoming fiftieth birthday...

Old Hubert lurks in the shadows. By the time you notice him he's already done quite a bit of damage, like destroying 50 to 70% of your dark matter neurons – and all with a smile.

Depression, economists would say, is a leading indicator of the presence of Old Hubert. It acts as a forerunner, an unconscious prescience of the encroaching illness. Here, Double-Click reveals his groundbreaking anticyclonic system based on the following principle:

 "Either I complain today about feeling worse than yesterday, and it won't do me much good for tomorrow will be even worse, and so will the day after and the day after that again,

"or I am thankful that I'm feeling better today than tomorrow, for tomorrow I will be better still than the following day."

***

As he finishes posting about his anticyclonic system on his blog, Double-Click feels a niggle creeping up on him. True, he is often in a great mood now that he focuses more on the present day than before and makes the most of every moment, but he is also highly conscious of the limits of his happy-go-lucky approach to life, especially when Old Hubert is lurking – ready to pounce and push him under at the first sign of fatigue.

L-Dopa can only do so much to help him deal with the downsides of his condition. And sometimes, it's clearly out of its depth.

IS IT DEPRESSION THAT'S MAKING ME ILL?
OR MY DISEASE THAT'S MAKING ME DEPRESSED?
-THEY'RE BOTH EXHAUSTING!
GABS.

20. <u>L-DOPA</u>

L-Dopa is not the official Tour de France drink; it's just a drug containing dopamine.

***

Son of P...arkin, the Mind-boggling Blog

<u>Drug Addiction</u>

Dopamine is a protein. Before he was diagnosed, Double-Click knew nothing about it, but it has since become an increasingly invasive part of his life.

Dopamine (DA) is a neurotransmitter. Mainly produced in the dark matter, it plays an essential role as final modulator of the motor and psychological outputs.

Double-Click reflects on this. Although he never was a chemistry whiz-kid, he understands that dopamine secretion – by only 1% of his neurons – is as essential to his brain as oxygen to his lungs or as a frothy head to a beer.

Unfortunately, ingesting is not the same as secreting. The brain is equivalent to the human body's Pentagon: a command center with secured access. When dopamine comes from an external source, it can't go past the blood-brain barrier – it is repelled at the brain's gates like an unwelcome migrant. To bypass this hurdle, researchers disguised the ungainly external dopamine as L-Dopa, endowing it with the looks of Brigitte Bardot in And God Created Woman and Isabelle Adjani's smoldering gaze in One Deadly Summer. So much so that the new-look L-Dopa sailed through every security check the second time around. That's when the miracle happened: L-Dopa suffused Double-Click's neurons with dopamine, and a sense of well-being washed over Double-Click, who felt at one again with his muscles and gestures – and with the world around him.

The role of dopamine as a neurotransmitter was discovered by the Swedish scientists Arvid Carlsson and

Nils-Äke Hillarp in 1958. Despite the billions of dollars invested in research worldwide, no worthy successor has been found to it since – such as a magic protein compound that would treat the root cause of the disease and not just the symptoms. So, for the time being, Double-Click makes do with getting his legal fix at regular hours.

***

L-Dopa became a part of Double-Click's family a few years ago, when he was working much longer hours than today. He used to leave early in the mornings and come home late in the evenings – at the time, Old Hubert still had little impact on his professional and personal lives.

Back then, L-Dopa was a rather discreet and casual companion that spent most of its time happily ensconced in a kitchen drawer. It was a strategic place, the epicenter of family life. Double-Click's children were all still going to school and often brought friends home. They would have fun while eating delicious snacks. Any excuse was good for organizing parties at home for the kids. Aure was a great host to all of them – and she loved making them feel welcome. Used to more senior settings, L-Dopa was bathing in an elixir of youth.

21. <u>EYE WIDE SHUT</u>

When Double-Click was a teenager, literary critics were laudatory of Georges Perec's virtuoso novel A Void.

The original French title of A Void is La Disparition, meaning 'the disappearance'. One can read the book's few hundred pages in full without noticing that the author never used the letter 'e', neither in the title nor anywhere else, whereas it was used nearly fifty times to write these two paragraphs alone.

It's the same thing with Old Hubert, Double-Click tells himself; your whole body is affected. You're fully aware of the changes caused by the pathology both physically and psychologically.

But you try your best to hide them from the people around you, and most of the time no one notices, including the ones closest to you. You work real hard to keep your symptoms at bay.

Because they cause a schism between you and the normal world, that of the healthy. This is one of the trickiest parts I have to deal with in my struggle, thinks Double-Click. I must do everything in my power to suppress my symptoms, because when they appear out of the blue they destabilize me and make me vulnerable. That's how I feel about them, in any case. But another reason why I want to talk about them is to show the people around me how frustrating and even humiliating

Old Hubert can be to me, so they understand why I need to exorcise that feeling.

A paradox in itself: to conceal without hiding.

***

When Double-Click shared his metaphor with Aure, she laughed. And when he mentioned the word 'disappearance', she recalled his propensity to disappear in the middle of a conversation or meal – as if he were suddenly sucked away. She thinks he is listening, but he is elsewhere. Double-Click should talk to Mona about it, she knows how to get attention. What is her secret?

Suddenly, she stops talking. She will be late for her appointment, and she hates being late. She leaves without him noticing.

***

Deep in thought, Double-Click reflects on how hard it is for him to hide his symptoms now. The diagnosis came as a shock at first. He had to come to terms with its psychological impact and start to come to grips with his own mortality and vulnerability.

His attitude toward other people changed radically. He still felt protective of Aure and the children, but when Old Hubert reared its ugly head and destabilized him, he sought to protect himself, either by venting his anxiety with Aure or by looking for signs of support and love from his children. And that was new. He didn't like to admit it, but it had become his reality.

He changed in the eyes of other people too; they no longer saw him as invincible and successful in every situation. He was normal now.

He decided to take a step back at work when he realized he was no longer primus inter pares. He was not bitter over it: Old Hubert had altered his priorities. Success was no longer his goal; his number-one focus now was finding the energy and time to fight the disease.

A period of relative calm followed the few months of post-traumatic depression. It lasted while he could still

conceal his symptoms, but they had not disappeared –
L-dopa may have given him that illusion, but Old Hubert
had been lurking in wait all along. And although Double-
Click was fighting it every second of every day, his
energy was beginning to fade.

That's when Double-Click realized he would have no
choice but to face his disease and its consequences, no
matter how hard he tried to brush them off and play
down their physical impact. He would have to deal with
the ABCs of symptoms, the alphabet Old Hubert uses to
write your story a few years after his first intrusion.

22. <u>THE ABC OF SYMPTOMS</u>

Double-Click is finding it increasingly difficult to pretend he is just like everyone else.

He dutifully takes his fix with the regularity of a Swiss cuckoo clock and gets manipulated by Slim twice a week. He can tell the honeymoon period is over. Honeymoon? The majority of Parkinson's patients who start treatment with L-dopa experience a significant improvement in symptoms. However, the effect of the drug tends to fade over time. That's why the beginning of treatment is compared to a honeymoon.

Double-Click wonders who came up with the concept of a honeymoon, as if one got married to Old Hubert out of love when it's more like a forced marriage 'for better or for worse' – without a divorce option.

Old Hubert is not a lone wolf, he has three stooges called Aki, Bobbing Bob, and Carcan: they're the ABC of symptoms.

***

Chinese Portraits

Aki is Japanese, but her name comes from the Greek akinesia which means 'without movement'. She recently had her Chinese portrait done despite the age-old Sino-Japanese conflict.

If she were an animal, she would be a turtle; if she were a book, she would be In praise of slowness; if she were a font, she would be Micrographia; and if she were a sport, she would be cricket. Aki is what is called a narcissistic pervert. She gets her kicks from blocking yours and only reaches ecstasy when you fall.

Bobbing Bob is a bit of a pig-latin guy. He's the most famous of the trio, but maybe not the most embarrassing one. If he were an animal, he'd be a mad cow; if he were a band, he'd be REM; if he were a scale, he'd be Richter's; if he were a film, he'd be The Shining; if he were a voice, he'd be Julien Clerc's. Bobbing Bob loves making you tremble just when you want to hide your emotion, which never fails to create an awkward moment between you and your interlocutor.

Carcan is Canadian, he has founded an organization to boycott gymnastics at the Olympic Games. If he were an animal, he'd be a razor clam; if he were a job, he'd be a sandwich-board man; if he were a phrase, he would be 'stiff as a lamppost'; and if he were a monument, he'd be the Leaning Tower of Pisa. Carcan hates to be challenged. He loves to stiffen your muscles just when Aki attacks your coordination. For example, he takes perverse pleasure in having you knock your chair over at a concert just as you try to slip away unnoticed.

'I'd rather tremble for the health of others than for my own. It hurts less.'

Bobbing Bob loves this quote by Tristan Bernard. He sees himself as the lead character among the ABC of symptoms trio. He best represents the pathology. Unlike immobility and slowness, unlike rigidity and stiffness which can be either positive, neutral, or negative, having the shakes invariably conveys a sense of weakness and inferiority.

Shaking with cold, fear, shame, rage, fury, shaking with joy and pleasure all mean a loss of self-control, an inability to channel emotions. In a society where one ought to have control over oneself, to shake is an admission of weakness, of submission to an event or a person.

Bobbing Bob is aware of the pity or laughter he triggers. "When I make Double-Click shake, everyone looks away," he says, before adding: "When that happens, I can tell Double-Click wishes he could just disappear."

***

"You're overdoing it a little, Bobbing Bob," says Double-Click.

"Watch CNN," comes the answer, "you're in for a surprise!"

"All right, I will," Double-Click replies, unconvinced.

23. <u>YOGA AND MEDITATION</u>

After much coaxing from Aure, Slim, and Mona, and with much grumbling, Double-Click gave yoga and meditation a go. He thought there might be something in it for him if three bright people encouraged him to try it.

And so here he is, lying on the floor in the large living room-turned-ashram on Avenue de la Bourdonnais, listening to the hypnotic voice of his instructor, renamed Guru for the occasion and missioned with the difficult task of taking him from darkness to light.

Aki, Bobbing Bob, and Carcan have long awaited this moment. They are ready as can be – they've left nothing to chance. As soon as Double-Click tries to make a move, they revel in stymying it, especially Carcan since Double-Click was never flexible and is now paying the price for it.

While his guru performs the exercises with ease, his own attempts lack flexibility and range. In turn, he tries the Cobra, the Claw, the Half-candle, the Twist, the Triangle, the Plow, the Candle, the Fish, the Tree, the Bow, the Grasshopper, and so on. The first class ends with a long series of abdominal breathing that leave him knocked out and half-asleep like an upturned crocodile whose brain is no longer irrigated.

The next sessions are less painful; in fact, they get increasingly pleasant and even effective. They don't slow down Old Hubert's inescapable progress, but they do make him feel better.

As for meditation, although it was quite popular, he knew even less about it. It involved the same hypnotic voice and the same obedience to the guru's orders. It was all about learning to stay still and silent. Silence is fine; but staying still when Bobbing Bob takes control of your fingers and Carcan contracts the muscle of your toe until it goes into spasms is a whole different ballgame.

Double-Click was happy when the thirty minutes of meditation ended, and even happier when he realized that the other participants had found it a challenge too. Still, he had been drawn to the session's invitation to live in the present, so essential when the past stirs nostalgia and the future breeds anxiety.

Double-Click found himself telling his incredulous and highly amused children how enjoyable tasting a single grape in more than five minutes can be, and how it awakens his senses. What a change from his old food-swallowing habits close to bingeing! It may sound funny, but it made Double-Click feel immediately better, and now he sometimes resorts to meditation to fend off the occasional bout of anger or irritation.

***

Upon seeing that Double-Click enrolled in the same meditation class as her, Mona recalls his old thought system during their first meeting at La Salpêtrière. And although his progress makes her feel both surprised and delighted, she is not sure what posture to adopt. Is she supposed to remain distant as an analyst should or, since they're on neutral ground, can she engage in dialogue with him?

Double-Click solves her quandary by starting a conversation with her, telling her how good he feels after the meditation class. He confides his surprise at how hard it is to focus on the here and now and make the most of all the little things we usually take for granted. He even goes as far as disclosing the changes he is experiencing, both physically and in the way he experiences things. He concludes by saying "I'm sure we will have the opportunity to discuss it further, elsewhere." Then he walks away, hindered by his right leg.

24. <u>NEW APPROACHES</u>

Meanwhile, researchers worldwide keep on searching.
Their imagination is limitless.

*****

Son of P…arkin, the Mind-boggling Blog

<u>Tai Chi Chuan or French Billiards?</u>

While some people risk their lives collecting squalamine,
a substance found in shark livers known for its
extraordinary results in the treatment of neurological
disorders in particular, others test the benefits of Tai-
Chi-Chuan: according to an American study published in
the latest issue of the New England Journal of Medicine,
'Tai-Chi-Chuan seems to alleviate balance disorders in
Parkinson's sufferers'.

Still others – probably the most daring of all – trade a
few brain cells for a joint in the name of science: 'The

benefits of cannabis include reduction in resting tremor, alleviation of bradykinesia- and dyskinesia-induced Levodopa, appetite stimulation, and improved sleep quality'. Nothing new under the sun as far as cannabis is concerned.

In his personal quest for scientific progress, Double-Click finds all these experiments quite inspirational. He has noticed that his symptoms tend to decrease significantly in given circumstances that ought to be tested on a larger group of patients. Winetasting, for example: different vintages (1929, 1945, 1971, 2005) of Domaine de la Romanée Conti grands crus (Romanée Conti, La Tâche, Romanée Saint-Vivant, Grand Echezeaux, etc.) seem to improve his olfactory sense and increase his deep sleep cycle. A vacation in Brazil during the last World Cup both improved his erectile function and caused excessive sweating. Playing French billiards, and especially winning against his old friend Phil, reduced Double-Click's behavioral problems, hypersexual impulses, and akinetic episodes.

And although Double-Click often talks about these new therapeutic approaches with his neurologist, it doesn't make much difference.

Phil is Double-Click's oldest friend. The two sniggering teens first met in ninth grade and soon became fast friends.

Phil and Double-Click would find creative ways to kill time, such as building and selling small Morse code messaging devices that were supposed to share the answers with the whole class during multiple-choice quizzes. The end result didn't quite live up to expectations though. The code signals were distorted by the high numbers of messages sent across the classroom at the same time.

One day, Double-Click had a crazy idea: throwing firecrackers at the open-top riverboats that cruised the Seine under the Bir Hakeim bridge. His wicked joy at watching the Japanese tourists dive for cover as the crackers went off was interrupted by the police. He had no choice but to throw his last firecrackers into the river.

In the current climate of hysteria, Phil mused, Double-Click would have been locked away in Guantánamo Bay and stripped of his Alsatian nationality.

All this to say that the pair go back a long way. Double-Click appreciates Phil's wry sense of humor and his propensity to 'tell it as it is'. As for Phil, he admires Double-Click's optimism, entrepreneurial drive, professional success, and happy family.

When Double-Click confided about Old Hubert, Phil heard the sadness in his voice and realized that his own vision of the world was not quite dark enough. He tried to comfort his friend with a joke, but it fell flat because he himself was too affected by the news. Double-Click smiled absently.

Phil decided to spend more time with Double-Click. He could tell his friend was getting better as the months went by. Although he was not fully back to his old triumphant self yet, Double-Click showed a renewed interest in his business and family. His sense of humor was coming back too: when he made a joke about his awkward gait, Phil knew it was a good sign – it also meant that he, too, was allowed to make fun of Old Hubert, and with Double-Click's blessing to boot. It goes without saying that he had a field day with it!

Old Hubert had tried to separate them, in vain. Actually, it had reinforced their bond. No one, nothing could interfere with their exclusive friendship.

***

Double-Click rediscovered Phil's dark wit with glee. His friend had developed a subtle and nuanced sense of humor that excelled at rooting out and dismantling all forms of conformism. With him, Double-Click didn't feel at all self-conscious about his slight limp or weakening voice.

Later, Double-Click read a few tweets by his friend that set his day off to a good start. Here is one of them:

'As the ceremony draws to an end, one of Johnny Hallyday's ex-wives will be chosen to be sacrificed and buried with him. Vote by texting 'Sylvie' or 'Nath' to 912.

'My dear Phil, Double-Click said to himself, at least you shook me out of my dark thoughts.

25. <u>RUMORS</u>

Double-Click decides to take Bobbing Bob's advice. He sits on his couch and switches on the bizarre, garish TV channel whose banner spouts a constant stream of world news and stock prices. He learns that during his 2016 campaign, Trump could not resist the lure of a weapon of mass destruction that was easy to manufacture and didn't require advanced technology: 'Parkinson's rumors'.

***

Son of P...arkin, the Mind-boggling Blog

On the Correct Usage of Rumors

To quote Knowckers.org, 'It appears that Hillary Rodham Clinton is receiving Levodopa as treatment for a Parkinson's syndrome that has been evolving over the past ten years'.

And it gets more specific: 'The impact on motor skills can lead to walking difficulties that necessitate the assistance of both the doctor in charge of monitoring Mrs. Clinton's steps, Dr. Lisa Bardack, and a black aide (sic) in helping her climb a flight of stairs, for example.

'In addition – and not to mention the three times she fell because of a balance disorder specific to this neurodegenerative disease – she suffers from dysphagia that leads to severe coughing fits and is thus likely to develop aspiration pneumonia, as it actually happened on September 9 in Cleveland. A complication that could have been fatal.'

In other words, dear American voters, don't bother voting for Hillary, she'll be dead in a few days anyway. But did the new POTUS take advantage of this rumor?

Let's take a look at the OBS magazine of July 24, 2016:

'Last week, Donald Trump's spokeswoman Katrina Pierson said on television that Hillary Clinton has dysphasia (speech impairment). And although Donald Trump never openly spread the rumor, he did drop a few hints at a foreign policy meeting: "[Hillary Clinton] lacks the mental and physical stamina to take on ISIS and all of the many adversaries we face.'

On Saturday, August 20, he tweeted: 'Where's Hillary? Sleeping!'

"So subtle! I guess Trump should have read what I wrote about sleep on my blog," Double-Click exclaims.

Luckily, we wouldn't tolerate that kind of behavior here in France! Our political system is too civilized for this. Or is it, really? On August 26, 2015, the French periodical 20 minutes published: 'At 69, the oldest member of the government Laurent Fabius made a quick recovery. But his fainting spell revived rumors about his state of health, and about Parkinson's in particular'.

"Parkinson's? Now, that's news to me. Do I look like I'm shaking?" he told Le Monde.

***

Interesting, thinks Double-Click, it's always Bobbing Bob who is used to caricature Old Hubert. True enough, the tremors ruin everything: caring for one's family, working, having fun, and even laughing at the irony of it all.

It's physio time. Double-Click takes a shower and puts on his shorts, feeling a little guilty for not having done any of the exercises Slim asked him to do last time.

As Double-Click stretches his triceps, psoas, pectorals, and adductors, he feels a searing pain in his right leg's quadriceps – it's Carcan reminding him that he hates being woken up without warning.

Slim rings the bell. Double-Click opens the door, absentminded, thinking about that intriguing Le Monde article on jealousy. He will post an excerpt from it on his blog.

Are things even worse than I care to admit? he wonders while getting ready for his physio.

26. <u>DR. HOUSE VS OTHELLO</u>

Double-Click didn't sleep well, and now the ABC of Symptoms is teasing him. His body is aching and further evading him.

Sure, he has lost some of his heyday looks, but he is not one to take it lying down! Whenever unease rears its head, he either goes to see Mona or immerses himself in an episode (or two) of Dr. House.

Hugh Laurie is so cool! The way he turned his 'Tower of Pisa' posture, bad limp, and blatant misanthropy into fatal weapons of seduction is just brilliant.

Should I grow a beard? wonders Double-Click.

But it's not that simple for him. Not only does he lack Gregory H.'s sadistic cynicism, but his gorgeous wife Aure seems unmarred by the passage of time – she's a real stunner. As a result, Double-Click develops a condition known as the 'Othello syndrome', a delusional disorder brilliantly described in Le Monde.

***

Son of P...arkin, the Mind-boggling Blog

<u>The Jealous Man Who Once Made Others Jealous</u>

'On August 16, 2017, Cortex magazine published an article online in which British clinicians report a rare side effect that can be potentially harmful to couples in patients treated for Parkinson's disease. Known as Othello Syndrome, this complication was named after William Shakespeare's tragedy'.

Le Monde mentions two instances of this syndrome:

'A 51-year-old patient developed a severe case of Othello Syndrome, as well as hypersexuality and visual hallucinations, one month after being administered dopaminergic drugs (ropinirole). He became convinced that his wife was sleeping with other men, including his own son. He went as far as to hire a private investigator to follow his wife and had his home wired, making holes in the walls and removing floorboards to install microphones.'

Double-Click did a bit of research and found out that the patient's name was Laius, his wife was Jocasta, and that after sleeping with his mother their son Oedipus was about to kill his father. Turns out Ropinirole had nothing to do with any of this.

'A 47-year-old patient showed signs of delusional jealousy after she started taking ropinirole. The delirium led to a shopping addiction and visual hallucinations. She was certain that her husband was cheating on her with several other women, including her best friends. After they broke up, she convinced herself her husband was harassing her. she even changed the locks because she thought he was trying to get into the house.'

And even if her husband did get closer to her best friends, he can't be cheating on her now since they are divorced...

Double-Click realizes that he does get a bit jealous at times. But has that got anything to do with the aforementioned infamous syndrome? His wife is attractive. Other men are really courting her. Nothing delusional about it. In his great wisdom, and since he can't bring himself to choke his own wife (Shakespeare didn't do things by halves) or kill himself there and then, he takes refuge in a poem.

I once was 'man adroit'
Now I am maladroit
Some will call it clumsy
That's when pain fills my body
It makes me feel gauche
I try to move and I flush
As my limbs evade my command
They live a life of their own
And that has me thrown

Make me laugh, House
Make me think of something else
I say goodbye to the blues
And to my jealous views
As I listen to Carmen
The beautiful Andalusian

Nestled in the arms

Of my beloved wife

Amen

***

Double-Click's mother Odette was quite amused by the chapter on Oedipus. Of course, Double-Click is a loving son who has never expressed the desire to marry her nor attempted to kill his father. Still, this myth – a founding principle of psychoanalysis – makes her feel rejuvenated.

After she had finished – supposing one ever finishes – raising Double-Click and his three sisters, she went back to university to study psychology.

She found her calling as a psychologist when her eldest daughter Olga, who always signed her drawings with a little rabbit in the bottom-right corner of the sheet, added a second rabbit and then a third one to her signature after the birth of each of her two sisters.

As chance would have it, a few years later she was working in the child psychology department of La Salpêtrière, the same hospital where Double-Click got his first appointment with Mona.

The news of Double-Click's diagnosis confused her. Her protective instinct as a mother wasn't ready for it, and she couldn't quite find the words to address the issue. Actually, she has always found it hard to talk about problems. She likes to be seen as a strong mother and, to her, emotional displays are akin to losing control. They're an admission of weakness. At Double-Click's wedding, she had taken a mild tranquillizer before walking her son to the altar. No way was she going to let emotion overwhelm her!

Twenty-five years later, while on a family trip to Sicily, she indulged in a glass of the true Italian bitter liqueur Fernet-Branca – her guilty pleasure – as she and Double-Click stayed up late talking. They chatted about this and that for a while, then, a little tipsy, she finally dared to ask him how he was. Her direct question caught him off guard.

They were discussing treatments and their effectiveness when she suddenly fell silent, cutting the conversation short. Her blue eyes welled up. She looked at him in that special way a mother looks at her son and said: "I wish Old Hubert had chosen me instead of you. It would have been more natural..."

Although her guilt was unfounded, it was as irrepressible and futile as Double-Click's over believing his illness was the cause of her sorrow. Odette's confession came as a relief, further helped by another round of Fernet-Branca.

It would help them sleep, too;

27. <u>IGUAZÚ</u>

Double-Click goes to the dentist to have a crown placed on a hard-to reach tooth. In her pink coat, the young assistant looks like Little Pink Riding Hood (is he hallucinating?). The Chief Dentist is wearing a blue coat. In a didactic tone, he instructs her to keep the operating area dry.

"For the dental cement to harden in the best conditions."

The assistant seems panicky, on the verge of a nervous breakdown (some might even say burnout) from wanting to please her boss but not being able to; indeed, the saliva vacuum tube stuck between Double-Click's cheek and lower jaw is clearly not up to snuff: it was not designed to absorb a water flow of Iguazú Falls magnitude in the aftermath of climate-change Amazonian downpours.

So, when the suction tube stopped functioning, the saliva tsunami that swept Double-Click, the Chief Dentist, his assistant, and the practice away threatened to flood all of Paris.

Double-Click wakes up in a sweat. What a horrid nightmare! Can't be true – or can it? Let's hear the experts on this.

'Sialorrhea (excessive drooling) is a common symptom of Parkinson's disease. But contrary to appearances, it is generally not caused by hypersalivation but by the patient's inability to swallow his saliva fast enough to prevent drooling. Consequences include speech disorders and lower self-confidence, which can lead to social isolation.'

Social isolation. No less. Not exactly worth drooling over, though. In any case, Double-Click wants to reassure the reader, he doesn't resemble Big Bad Wolf looking at Little Red Riding Hood yet.

***

Son of P…arkin, the Mind-boggling Blog

<u>Who Am I (2)</u>

I am a film written and directed by you.

Your scenarios are based on the highlights of your day and on long-lost memories.

You usually work at night, but paradoxically, if you feel tired during the day, you may also produce me during a nap.

You never pay your actors. Most of them are people you know, but sometimes you cast strange fictional characters. You often play the lead role.

Only you can give a rendition of me, one that is open to interpretation.

Sometimes I shed light on your current or past thoughts and anguish.

Well, according to the father of psychoanalysis.

I am the child of REM sleep, when your body is resting and your brain swings into action to put some order in all the data you've absorbed the previous day.

Although I'm often quite alluring, I can be scary too, like Double-Click's nightmare.

I am a dream.

***

Double-Click doesn't like his drooling dream, for it rings too close to his concerns: he fears his loved ones will be driven away by his increasingly conspicuous and unbecoming symptoms. Actually, he tends to amplify them. He'd give anything to be in Aure's head. How is she coping with Old Hubert being a part of their lives now? Is she like him, fighting against the intruder's sly attempts to separate them?

28. <u>MÉNAGE À TROIS</u>

A few days ago, a cramp seized Double-Click's leg while he was walking to work. He confessed to Aure about how episodes like this get him down. He even waxed melodramatic about it.

An attitude Aure despises above all else. After they had a chat about it, Double-Click felt bad. He apologized and swore on his mother's life that he would never wallow in self-pity again.

Then, all of a sudden, he burst into tears in his wife's arms, saying he did not deserve it, life was unfair, her life will be hell with him, he won't survive, she will divorce him and his children will get rid of him immediately afterwards, he will sink into dementia unless he dies first.

She looked at him, slightly stunned, then she gave him a smile and a kiss on the forehead. He stared back at her, slightly stunned too, and refrained from telling her that he found her moving like Kate Winslet in *Titanic*, passionate like Julie Christie in *Doctor Zhivago*, bewitching like Vivien Leigh in *Gone with the Wind*, innocent like Brigitte Fossey in *Forbidden Games*, touching like Omar Sy in *The Intouchables*.

Glad he managed to keep his mental monologue in check, he told himself she would have been better off if a law had been passed to regulate one's choice of a spouse. Indeed, one is much more cautious buying an apartment than choosing a husband.

When buying real estate, the seller must give the property's bill of health to the buyer. And it's serious business: Any asbestos in the lead? Do the termites keep warm with gas? What is the janitor's energy consumption rating? Is the dry rot fungus sanitized? Not to mention seismic hazards, floods, hurricanes, potential riots, and the rise of fanaticism.

But when it comes to choosing a husband, one relies on intuition and a few trial runs in the bedroom. That's all well and good, but what happens in case of hidden defects? Can the wife sue her mother-in-law? Can she ask the Church to annul the marriage? Does Amazon have a return policy for flawed hubbies? Not easy. Not easy at all.

Being a nurse was never part of her plan, let alone having to care for one single patient twenty-four seven. She never was into white coats and red crosses. Not to mention her Fine Arts degree, worlds apart from that of a nursing assistant. Plus, she has no intention of going back to college at this stage. Still, he thinks she may feel a little stuck now since she was the one who insisted that they marry under an unlimited prenup agreement. And to quote God's representative on earth: it is for better or for worse.

***

But Aure doesn't sees things that way. Double-Click has less symptoms than he thinks, even if they must feel huge to him as he experiences them from the inside. He must be trying hard to hide them, and it's working.

His situation reminds her of a pregnant woman focused on the baby she is the only one to know yet, while everyone else is still oblivious to the life-changing movements inside her. This is probably the happy equivalent of Double-Click's predicament.

His self-confidence and self-esteem have taken a hard knock. He has fallen off his pedestal and, although he remains strong-willed, the frustration and humiliation he endures get too much to handle sometimes.

At first, she couldn't bear the signs of weakness in his attitude. She thought he was wallowing in self-pity, especially as the symptoms were hardly noticeable. It was his strength of character, in particular, that had attracted her to begin with; now was the time to show it. Plus, she couldn't stand the thought of physical deterioration. She had always worked hard to ward off the signs of aging herself, with success. He had to make an effort too. Take up yoga, stretching, whatever.

He would get up in the middle of the night to read or write, then go back to bed even more tired and vulnerable. It would go from bad to worse, into a spiral. And his jealousy! She just couldn't handle it! But as time passed, she decided to take it upon herself and comfort him like a wretched child. He needs her now, oh so badly. He often declares his love to her these days. That's a big change from the past. She hadn't expected that much. It's true she had always sought to rebalance their relationship – but upward, not downward.

She did some research on the disease. She knows Old Hubert is slowly but surely undermining him, stealthily torpedoing his spirit. Chemical changes in the brain are gradually turning her once-triumphant husband into an emotional wreck. Crazy stuff! And unless science gets involved, she senses the worst is yet to come.

With the passing years, she has been wondering how she can be of help to him. Old Hubert is ever more encroaching upon their lives, playing havoc with Double-Clicking's gait and mood. It keeps him awake at night. It weakens his voice. It messes with his handwriting. In short, her husband is constantly suffering, and she feels helpless.

Sometimes she talks about it with her best friends. One of them settled in Switzerland a long time ago, another only recently moved to London. She misses their physical presence. Fortunately, her lifelong friend Joy drops by sometimes. She is great fun to be with, and Aure feels relaxed around her. She confides in Joy as if she were a sister, telling her there is no solution, they just have to deal with it. The best way to help Aure is to listen to her.

Double-Click's anguish increases in the evenings. Even though Aude wants to go to sleep, she makes the effort to answer him and reassure him. She thinks back to a time when she would have liked for him to listen to her, but she couldn't bring herself to ask him then. He was too busy with his work, oblivious to her silent need for dialogue.

In a surprising game of communicating vessels, Aure is like a late bloomer, finally freed from the burden of an absent father just when Double-Click needs protection from the insidious enemy inside.

She smiles as she muses that, at least, no one will take her Double-Click from her now. Life is not soft on the soft-hearted.

***

Double-Click senses what's going on, albeit in a confused way. He knows his relationship with Aure has changed. Sure, it's more balanced now, but as far as he's concerned it's also less comfortable. Of course, he is still protective whenever she feels down. He actually cherishes those moments when he can comfort her again, a feeling that's become too scarce for she seldom drops her guard these days.

He, on the other hand, often pours out his frustration to her. And the more he does so, the more distant she gets, the more he tries to show his love to her, and so on. He hates himself when that happens, when he senses her distance, because he does exactly the opposite of what's written in the first paragraph of the first chapter of *Seduction for Dummies*: 'If you want to be loved, remember it's better to arouse envy than pity!' But the more he thinks about it, the less he seems to succeed.

It's a real conundrum. Yes, he's totally confused. How is he supposed to be, or even feel, attractive when he's dragging Old Hubert everywhere he goes like a ball and chain? Yes, it's true, some days he gets jealous of any healthy being who makes Aure smile.

29. <u>NEYMAR/ROLY-POLY TOY</u>

But do his symptoms really change him as much as he thinks? Since science is all about measuring and comparing, neurologists from the world over have agreed on a unique measure to evaluate Parkinsonian syndromes.

***

Son of P...arkin, the Mind-boggling Blog

<u>UPDRS</u>

Called UPDRS (Unified Parkinson's Disease Rating Scale), this measure is to human tremors what the Richter Scale is to earthquakes. It comprises of six sections, hereafter detailed by Double-Click with enlightened comments.

Part I: evaluation of mentation, behavior, and mood (please kindly remove this funnel from your head).

Part II: self-evaluation of the activities of daily life, or ADLs (the meaningless things you do every day).

Part III: clinician-scored monitored motor evaluation (oil change, lubrication, oil filter, rip-off deal).

Part IV: complications of therapy in the week prior to the examination (prepare cribs for that one but don't get caught, exam rules are very strict).

Part V: Hoehn and Yahr staging of severity of Parkinson's disease (sadistic classification, detailed in the chapter 'Stages' so you're fully aware of what's awaiting you)

Part VI: Schwab and England ADL scale (researchers love to work in pairs. Still, a scale within a scale to measure the quality of life of one of Old Hubert's spouses seems a bit much).

Each section is based on questions and comments from the neurologist. For instance, Part III's 'Motor Evaluation' includes 14 questions rated on a 5-points scale, ranging from Normal (0) to Severe (4). Sounds quite scientific, does it not?

This moment of joy and bliss happens every three months and culminates with your very own report card. Please note that the higher your score, the more affected you are. Now an expert at deciphering the results, Double-Click is pleased to transpose them into five questions, just for you.

– Is your speech ability closer to Al Pacino's (0) or Buster Keaton's (4)?

– When you pull faces, do you look like Jim Carrey (0) or Buddha (4)?

– Can you move your hands fast like Punch (0), lively and agile, or like the policeman, slower than Punch whom he never catches (4)?

– When you play football, do you resemble Neymar (0) or a roly-poly toy (4)?

– And lastly, do you get up from a chair normally (0) or stiff as a post (4)?

Every three months, Double-Click repeats the same gestures in front of Doctor Z to assess Old Hubert's progression. Obediently executing the doctor's orders under his watchful gaze makes Double-Click feel like a hand puppet.

Dr. Z goes back to his calculations: so, let's say he sees around 15,000 patients over the course of his professional life. Given a life expectancy of approx. twenty years per patient and three visits per year, he performs 20*3*15,000 = 900,000 UPDRS tests in his career.

Impressive, he thinks proudly. A few more months at this rate and he would reach a million tests. *Double-Click may feel like a puppet, but I certainly get tired of the show sometimes.*

***

Double-Click goes home to find a comment in Indonesian on his blog. It was posted by Ocatarina, his assistant, while on a family vacation in Jakarta. Ocatarina is a great asset to the firm through her sheer hard work and intelligence.

He takes another look at the picture taken in Ksar Massa. Ocatarina was standing by herself, as if leaning against the frame of the photo, benevolently watching over her colleagues. He had danced the night away.

Seems like a lifetime ago.

30. <u>ON/OFF</u>

When Dr. Z asked him if he had any 'off' moments, Double-Click was puzzled – he'd never heard that expression before. And for good reason: he hadn't experienced those effects yet. But they eventually wormed their way into his daily life – insidiously, as always with Old Hubert. What are they? Let's ask him the question.

***

Son of P…arkin, the Mind-boggling Blog

<u>Alternating Current</u>

"After the 'honeymoon period,' treatment becomes less effective and involuntary movements occur. Periods of well-being ('on' periods) alternate with periods of blockage or involuntary movements ('off' periods)."

It dawns on Double-Click that Old Hubert can decide to turn him 'off' whenever the fancy takes him, as he would a radio or a toy.

By Jove! This is all the more unsettling as these 'off' periods seem to be more frequent and to last longer over time.

PS: Double-Click may appear calm on the surface, but AC power is not his thing. And contrary to the laws of electricity, he actually tends to blow a fuse when the 'off' period gets too intense. That's usually when he lets it all hang out and booms a thunderous *F... off!*

***

Before publishing a post on his blog, Double-Click likes to have its relevance assessed. Most of the time the task befalls Nadine, Eliane's super girlfriend, who was Double-Click's super girlfriend too when he started out in the Consulting business.

Nadine knows Double-Click quite well by now. In his first posts, he endeavored to address the thorny subject of Old Hubert with humor. He would search the Web for the latest discoveries and share them with his readers, whose numbers were growing beyond his expectations – and to his delight.

But now that she has gained his trust, in addition to proofreading his posts he turns to her for the topics he should address. Indeed, although they remain in keeping with the evolution of his pathology and his own personal feelings, the themes he picks have gradually lost their light-hearted tone. The more recent posts on jealousy and the 'On/Off' effects revealed Double-Click's current concerns. He found trying to mask the symptoms and their implacable progress quite disturbing, especially with Aure as she was the first to see his struggle. He was afraid of losing her esteem. He could barely stand his own image whenever Old Hubert was having virulent outbursts, which was happening more and more often. Nadine would try to reassure him, she would tell him that the people who love him don't calibrate the intensity of their affection and love according to his symptoms. She knows this for sure, but how can she make him see sense? Even Double-Click's most loyal friend Eliane, who understood how vulnerable he now felt, couldn't convince him that there was no room for fear or guilt with his family and friends. How could they help him get rid of his cruel and unfair self-judgment, and stop being so harsh on himself?

Perhaps being a bit more open in his blog about how he felt deep down would help. After all, his readers were probably going through similar feelings and doubts – as was evidenced by the blog's statistics and comments page. As it turned out, she had to stop Double-Click from switching to a daily post – hold your horses!

31. <u>**PATIENT / IMPATIENT**</u>

Double-Click had been through his first job interviews at a time when it was still easy for a young person to get work. It was so long ago – back in the prehistoric era. Not yet suffering from micrographia, he had sent beautiful handwritten letters to various companies.

That's how Double-Click realized he was impatient. His handwriting had given it away. Today still, his one goal whenever he starts something is to finish it, and his pathology is certainly not helping. This is further confirmed by Slim who reveals to Double-Click, while stretching his adductors, that 80% of his patients are impatient – and that he is the most impatient of his impatient patients.

Double-Click blames his impatience on the distorted vision of time imposed by his pathology. With the ABC of symptoms making your life a little more difficult each day, you feel hat you need to get moving ASAP and act now. It's a form of reverse procrastination: do today what you could do tomorrow. It's the epitome of impatience. But in his search for self-improvement, Double-Click has never been so impatient to be patient.

***

Slim and Double-Click are having lunch together, at long last. They had been wanting to for a while but couldn't find matching slots in their busy schedules.

Double-Click switched from processed foods to all-organic in the space of twenty-five years, thanks to Aure's gradual introduction of a strict-yet-tasty diet. Quinoa replaced potatoes, fresh gluten-filled baguettes gave way to wholegrain crispbread, white coffee turned into tea, red meat became steamed fish, and a mix of nuts and almonds exterminated the chocolate éclairs.

But on that particular day, Double-Click fully indulged in the transgression offered by his lunch with Slim: foie gras, ribsteak with chips, 'Bleu de Termignon' cheese, and profiteroles, the lot washed down with a magnum of Burgundy wine.

Of course, this type of diet slows L-Dopa along the blood-brain pathway. It ended up blocked by fat deposits for a while, before a good dose of baking soda finally broke them down.

Double-Click was thus not feeling his best when Slim broached the subject of his concern. To Slim's surprise, Double-Click was quite open about it: since he could no longer hide his disease, he wanted to adapt his strategy to Old Hubert to keep it in check.

Slim reminded him that sticking with his daily stretching routine would be a good start. Double-Click smiled and changed the subject: "Tell me, Slim, do you think it's normal for a collector like me to buy another pinball machine when I already have seventeen of them, or is it the sign of an addiction brought on by medication?"

Slim pretended he didn't hear.

32. <u>PRIMARY EFFECTS</u>

Double-Click is thrilled with his eighteenth pinball machine, but deep down, he wonders if he's not suffering from an addiction caused by the long-term intake of agonist and antagonist drugs. It's what his family think too.

The primary effect of these drugs is to prolong their action and limit fluctuations. The side effects include the appearance of addictions and obsessions. The following extreme cases were blown out of proportion by media channels that thrive on fear and sensationalism.

***

Son of P...arkin, the Mind-boggling Blog

<u>Rampant Addictions</u>

'Ruined by his anti-Parkinsonian medication!'

The following strange case was revealed by the newspaper *Le Parisien* last week. Blaming his betting addiction and ensuing financial ruin on his anti-Parkinsonian medication, a 60-year-old heavy gambler from Nîmes wants a refund of all the money he gambled.

'Before his disease, my client used to try his luck at games of chance like everyone else, maybe two or three times a year. His gambling addiction, which he kept secret from his family, began when he was prescribed the medication in question. He started borrowing money off everyone he knew to buy scratch cards. That's how he ended up squandering his life savings.'

According to neurologists, the compulsive propensity to collect everything and anything is also a fairly common form of addiction. Double-Click remembers reading about two very peculiar collections indeed.

One day, a youngish patient suddenly set out to collect the user's manuals for every single version of the camera 'Leica' since the company was founded in 1849.

Apparently, he's now only missing the instructions for the 'Leica I' released in 1927.

Another story tells of a retired gangster who became addicted to orange concrete mixers and their drivers after his encounter with Old Hubert. As these are hard to come by in shops, the wealthy collector commissioned a special team to hunt them down – but one of the kidnappings turned violent.

Did Double-Click buy his eighteenth pinball machine for the same reasons? By the way, it's a *Gottlieb Black Hole* – the connoisseurs will appreciate.

What's your opinion on this?

***

Max loves pinball. He's been playing it since he was a kid and got quite good at it. He even does something no one else thinks of: he reads the rules of the game, written in small print on the left side of the machine. This way, he can pick his targets instead of just sending the ball at random and pray it will score points. He also tries to keep it as high up as possible, as he noticed that it usually falls down the outlane somewhere in the lower part of the playing area. Naturally, he holds the highest scores on most pinball machines, except those claimed by Double-Click – whose feats no one has ever had the privilege to witness.

Max thinks his father might be addicted to pinball machines. Is it normal to have so many, and to spend so much time cleaning and repairing them? The other day, he came across his father's medication leaflet. He read the small print, more out of idleness than curiosity: 'Strong impulse to gamble excessively despite serious personal or family consequences; altered or increased sexual interest and behavior, uncontrollable excessive shopping or spending.'

I'm going to keep an eye on my Daddy. Just to make sure I don't end up with a baby sister! Max thinks to himself.

As for the money, his father's a bit of a big spender all right, but then again he's always been that way. Did he really buy Black Hole pinball out of compulsion? Max is perplexed.

"I know!" he exclaims all of a sudden. "I'll ask my friend at school about it, her parents are psychiatrists. Maybe she can enlighten me!". He types a short text on his phone and hits 'send': *Jewel, can I call you?*.

33. <u>SIDE EFFECTS</u>

The laboratories get paranoid with that kind of story. They cover themselves as much as they can to avoid being sued. When Double-Click read all the potential side effects of the patch that Dr. Z had just prescribed him, he began to feel a bit queasy.

***

Son of P...arkin, the Mind-boggling Blog

<u>Can Patient Information Leaflets Actually Make You Sick?</u>

Below, in brackets, are the side effects listed on the leaflet that comes with Neupro, an agonist often prescribed to augment the effects of L-Dopa.

Double-Click picks up the leaflet and reads: *Although not all of the following side effects may occur, if they do occur they may need immediate medical attention.*

Double-Click is sweating profusely. He feels weak and nauseous, on the verge of fainting *([...] A sudden drop in blood pressure accompanied by weakness, sweating or nausea).* He tries to pick himself up and focus on filling his forty EuroMillions lottery tickets, but his calves are starting to swell like inner tubes *([...] Compulsive or involuntary behavior such as gambling and excessive spending; high blood pressure; swelling of the legs, ankles or feet).* He watches Joan of Arc come down from the heavens and speak to him in English just when he thinks he's ballooned up to the size of a sumo *([...]*

Hallucinations involving the illusion of hearing, seeing or feeling something that doesn't really exist; weight gain).

He collapses from his chair, in the middle of dinner, his swollen legs shaking uncontrollably *([...] Symptoms may worsen, such as restless legs syndrome, fainting, and a tendency to fall asleep during daytime activities).*

Enough!

Here's a word of warning: if you are prone to psychosomatic reactions, never ever read the information leaflet that comes with your medication.

***

Joan of Arc is happy. Like Sir James Parkinson, her reputation is hard to shake off. The Virgin of Orleans! Not the best way to go unnoticed at parties. She could do with a different nickname.

Double-Click has shown great consideration for her. In fact, it's the first time anyone brought her down from the sky. When Sir James Parkinson comes out of his conference, she will tell him about Double-Click. Most mortals don't go beyond their preconceived ideas.

Meanwhile, he's dying to travel back in time, back to where he came from.

34. <u>SISTER SOULS</u>

Double-Click is the youngest of four children, the standard offspring quota for a married couple in France in the 1950s. His birth had been preceded by that of three daughters (Olga, Irina, and Macha). The arrival of a male child who would perpetuate his ancestors' family name ranked so high in the parental representation of the ideal household that Double-Click was almost called Désiré.

And so, Double-Click was born, quite unaware of the high expectations that already weighed upon him. Impatient as ever, and anxious to confirm to his mother that he was indeed a boy, he appeared three weeks earlier than expected. His zealousness had been rewarded with a spell in a state-of-the-art incubator.

He can't recall much of his sisters' welcome (who went by the name 'your-sisters' until he got his first lesson on possessive pronouns), but the photos taken at the time testify to their benevolent curiosity, much to the paternal joy of the photographer.

Double-Click was the only boy in a family of four children whose mother did not yet work, unlike their father. He became a die-hard gynophile, although one without any androphobic tendencies (in other words, he likes girls, he gets along with guys, but he doesn't get the two mixed up). He has fond memories of a protective, caring, funny, and loving childhood.

Double-Click basks in the warmth of this nostalgic plunge into the past. Although his relationships with his three sisters fluctuated to the whims and vagaries of life, each was unique and a great source of shared joy.

***

Son of P...arkin, the Mind-boggling Blog

<u>Family Portraits</u>

Olga is the eldest of his three sisters. With her, he likes to talk literature and observe the people around them. They often feel the same about what happens in their family circle and in the world at large.

Irina is the most reserved of the three. She and Double-Click don't need words to understand each other. She was a great help to him when Old Hubert first reared its head. Drawing on her forty years' experience as a hospital doctor in Paris, she gave him sound advice about how he should approach his new life, especially with his wife.

Macha is his big sister by two years. He used to climb into bed with her in the wee hours when he was a child. She is very caring. She took him on a few short but happy trips, including three days in San Francisco and seven days in Japan. Brief cultural teasers that leave you longing for more.

When Old Hubert unexpectedly invited himself into the family circle, Olga, Irina, and Macha didn't welcome him – in fact, they downright hated him. They lavished unreserved support upon Double-Click to try and counteract the wicked scheming of Old Hubert and his gang.

To arms, sisters! Form your battalions, let impure blood water our furrows.

They're my sister souls.

***

In *Son of P...arkin*, Olga carefully read Double-Click's description of their brother/sister relationship. Summing it up in just a paragraph, however dense, is a little short, she thought. He could have delved a little deeper into the recesses of his mind to unearth more revealing emotions. After all, they've known each other for over fifty years!

She organizes a lunch with her sisters so they can talk about it. After placing their orders, Irina and Macha pour their hearts out.

Olga thinks he could have talked about her jealousy, as the elder sibling, towards her infant brother – jealousy largely fueled by their parents' unbridled joy at having a boy at long last. Boy or girl, what difference did it make? Was Double-Click to blame for this macho one-upmanship? Come to think of it, he never played into it. All right, she is willing to absolve him of this crime that he did not commit – on one condition: he must stop portraying her as a hardcore intellectual. She's more than just a mind. He could at least mention their immediate and simple joy at being together.

Irina adds: "He portrays me as the discreet one, the one who hides her feelings. Do you really think I hid my feelings when I set out to seduce Pat? And the family doctor image is so conventional, so boring! What, you think I came out of the fetal envelope dressed in a white coat, perusing my internship papers? He could have mentioned that I learned Italian of late, so I could understand my neighbors in Puglia. He could have said how happy I feel when I sculpt. But no, of course, it's Olga who's the artist. Let's not challenge the stereotypes: the teacher can't be the doctor, now that wouldn't be right!"

"I got my fair share of stereotypes too," Macha chips in. "The usual spiel about Air France, and that's it. Nothing about my passion for photography, my boundless hospitality, my travels, my three children! I don't get my kicks out of dealing with angry passengers in the middle of an umpteenth pilot strike. Not even a word about his two older sisters' children. They don't matter either?"

"We like you, Double-Click, but you've got to get away from your introspection with Old Hubert. Everyone has problems, you know! Come on, cheer up, we forgive you, you're still our beloved little brother, but you gotta admit it feels good to kick preconceived ideas in the butt from time to time."

***

Double-Click wasn't expecting such a rebellion. He knew his post would trigger reactions, but he never thought they'd be so direct. Things might get tricky for him if Aure and the children start asking for more consideration too! Thinking Olga might be behind this mutiny, he decides to have a chat with her. In the meantime, he'll talk about his friends. They say getting up close and personal boosts traffic.

35. <u>DEAR RESEARCHERS</u>

Double-Click's friends are extraordinary people, of course. But above all, they are researchers without knowing it. They didn't know what to say at first – Old Hubert was a mystery to them. All they could do was give Double-Click friendly advice: "The main thing is to keep your spirits up," "It's important to see it as a battle," "Try and stay active, go out as much as you can," "I have a friend who had the same disease, he's still alive, you should follow his example."

But as Double-Click's friends started garnering information, they would fill him in on the latest news and experiences of fellow sufferers – which left him facing new dilemmas.

Should he have his dental fillings removed, as Nadine – whom he never thought would ever be interested in his teeth – suggested?

The mercury used in dental fillings could cause chronic diseases as serious as Alzheimer's and Parkinson's.

Should he fast according to the recent recommendations of his old friend Gandhi and his cousin France? Researchers at the National Institute on Aging in Baltimore claim to have found evidence that *fasting for one or two days a week could protect the brain from some of the worst effects of Alzheimer's, Parkinson's, and other disorders.*

Should he take antioxidant supplements, as Gandhi suggested?

Research shows that dopamine-producing nerve cells may be disappearing due to oxidation. Thus, powerful antioxidants could play a beneficial role.

All right. But wouldn't it be easier to just down a bottle of anti-rust solution? Case closed, moving on.

"Why don't you try Ayurveda?" his new boss ventured one day. Double-Click hadn't expected him to express such concern.

Ayurveda is based on the principle of achieving balance between the three main Doshas, or body energies: Vata, Pitta, and Kapha.

Sounds like fun!

"Praying would do you good," said his great friend Courrèges. No doubt his loyal, trusted, and supportive friend Duke would agree.

'At sunset, the people brought to Jesus all who had various kinds of sickness, and laying his hands on each one, he healed them.' (Luke 4:40).

He doesn't mind praying, actually. You never know, it all else fails here on earth, it might just do the trick with Saint Peter.

Kylian suggested laughter therapy. That was a few months ago; he should now be pleased to see that Double-Click followed his advice. Grilladin sang the praises of football, a game he used to play. Now he just watches it from the stands.

Phil cracks the odd joke about pain. "You won't be laughing so much when your back hurts."

The discreet T & A offered to help Double-Click in a way that he cannot disclose here.

Isis, who knows the medication industry like the back of her hand, got him stuff that can only be found in Switzerland (it would cost too much to reimburse in France) and kept him informed on the latest developments.

That's what friendship is about. And it is bound to work, as foreseen by the Shadoks in their great wisdom: 'The more you fail, the more you have a chance that it will work in the end.'

And there certainly are plenty of fails in the research on Old Hubert...

***

Courrèges opens the door to Germain and Paige, who – figuratively – dropped their drones and sculptures, respectively, to come to dinner. Grilladin arrives first, alone. He left Ode to her search engine. Then the Of-the-Nuts show up, with Gandhi in their stride. They've just taken the last free street parking spaces, at the expense of the Gailles who are running a bit late. Gaillette is wearing a dress with parrot motifs.

Courrèges and Oscar are as welcoming as they are idle. It's easy to entertain guests when that's all you have to do, beside raising six children, managing and developing an enterprise dedicated to the art of communication and anticipating societal upheavals, tending to parish duties, objectifying gender inequality, giving real meaning to financial jobs, creating a new political party in the center of the left of the right, watching the Formula 1 Grand Prix, and so on and so forth.

They are happy to be together. They talk about everything and nothing, recall fond memories, share their fears, hopes, and joys. And of course, like all good friends, they talk about the others. What could be more enjoyable than a friendly discussion about the others, whose only wrong tonight is their absence? They chat happily.

It's now Double-Click and Aure's turn. Everyone likes them. They are so different, and yet they get along so well. Has anyone ever heard them argue? Nope. Inviting them for the holidays is always a pleasure. Asking them for a favor usually meets a yes – if they can help, they will. I'm getting bored with this conversation. Aren't you?

"How's his disease evolving?"

"He told me it was more of a burden now," says Courrèges, who had lunch with Double-Click the previous week. "He didn't dwell on it, but he said it wasn't easy."

"Well, they do travel a lot. You're right, it's like an obsession. Peru last summer, Burma next winter. No wonder he's tired, what with the visits and the time difference."

"Not to mention last week when he went to see a football match in Barcelona. 24 hours, round trip. He's not being reasonable, if you ask me."

"Travel is one thing. Sure, he's overdoing it, but what makes it worse is that he won't listen to advice. You think he pays attention, but he doesn't. He can be a bit of a hypocrite at times, always trying to avoid conflict. It would be so much easier if he just said he doesn't agree with us."

"It's true, he's a great guy, but he tends to think he's smarter than the rest of us."

"I agree," adds another guest. "I brought him some powerful antioxidant supplements from Germany. You can't get them here. I bet you he hasn't taken them. Of course, Aure and her obsession with natural foods isn't helping. Remember when she would only give soy milk to her children?"

"Yeah, unbelievable. She even gave them almond milk. When Anaïs was born, she had special bottle teats sent over from the US."

Everyone laughs, just like the Double-Clicks would too in similar circumstances.

"Still, they're going through a rough time. They're not doing so badly after all," concludes Courrèges.

"Better than the Anders anyway. Have you heard? They divorced via Facebook."

"No way! Are you kidding? I'd understand if they'd sent a text, but laying it all bare on Facebook!"

"It doesn't surprise me that much, mind you."

And so on.

***

Double-Click's ears, which had been ringing again, pop suddenly. Silence at last.

"That noise gets annoying at times," he says.

"Maybe Old Hubert's got nothing to do with it," replies Aure.

36. <u>STAGES</u>

When the diagnosis struck, Double-Click wanted to know what was in store for him in the years to come. That's how he came across the Hoehn and Yahr Scale. When he first read it, he found it so cold and clinical that he was afraid to go through it again. But running a blog – and entertaining the hope of reward – calls for certain sacrifices.

***

Son of P...arkin, the Mind-boggling Blog

<u>Stage 0 Wasn't so Bad After All</u>

Hoehn and Yahr don't beat about the bush in their description of the fate awaiting Double-Click at the hands of Old Hubert. And the worst part is, their predictions are turning out to be true.

Stage 0: No sign of Parkinson's disease (You're still blissfully unaware of the existence of Old Hubert – you don't know how good you have it).

Stage I: Unilateral involvement only, usually with minimal or no functional disability (the nagging pain in the shoulder, feeling down).

Stage II: Bilateral or midline involvement without impairment of balance (the diagnosis is still ringing in your ears, you're processing the shock, but Dr. Z introduced you to L-Dopa so everyday life is not a real struggle yet).

Stage III: Mild to moderate bilateral disease; some postural instability; physically independent. This shows when the patient changes direction or is pushed while standing with his feet together (things are starting to go downhill).

Stage IV: Severe disability; still able to walk or stand unassisted, but with great difficulty, partial loss of autonomy (why don't we change the subject).

Stage V: Confinement to bed or wheelchair unless aided (easy, tiger).

***

Sir James Parkinson finally managed to have a chat with Alois Alzheimer, who was born in 1864 – forty years after his own death. He tells Alois that his name is even scarier than his own. Alois agrees, and admits that maybe he shouldn't have given his lecture at the 37th Conference of Southwest German Psychiatrists in Tübingen, on 4 November 1906. He, who died from the complications of rheumatic fever in 1915, now embodies the symptoms of his patient Auguste Deter's disease.

"Alzheimer's disease should be called Deter's disease!"

Hans Gerhard Creutzfeldt and Alfons Maria Jakob, whom he both met at the Royal Psychiatric Hospital, nod in approval. They too had managed to escape the dreaded personification syndrome until that wretched Mad Cow Disease broke out in the early 1990s and propelled them into the limelight. And look who's joining the debate – good old George Huntington!

"The notion of prejudice no longer applies up here in heaven," Sir James goes on, "but I do appreciate Double-Click's attempt at rehabilitating my name."

"Double-Click? Who is that?" asks Alois, surprised.

"A Frenchman who fights for the ailing to be better respected. No an easy task, believe me."

37. <u>SAME PLAYER SHOOT AGAIN</u>

Double-Click is totally addicted to pinball machines, which also happen to be his favorite antidepressant.

The undivided pleasure he feels whenever he launches the ball into play invariably brings about a hint of nostalgia. The rolling ball sends him down memory lane, back to when he used to play hooky from high school with Phil while his 'Première S' classmates listened to the explanations of their physics teacher Gobi, whose mouth used to freeze wide open whenever a complex demonstration occupied his brain.

To think that the pinball machines' 120 kg worth of intricate electronic and mechanical parts, complete with cables and relays, would now fit into a microprocessor weighing less than one gram! Unfortunately, these robust but complex machines are known to break down and ruin your best scores.

Although Double-Click longed to try and repair them, he was hesitant at first. But curiosity got the better of him, and after spending long mornings working on them – courtesy of his bygone auroral sleep – he is now capable of taking apart and reassembling the impressive machines from scratch. And then, one day, *Eureka!* It hit him. Double-Click's obstinate curiosity was fueled by an unconscious desire to repair himself.

He disassembles Fronton and Caisson, revealing the brain and the internal organs connected by wires (neurons) and electrical excitations caused by different current forces; the sensors (targets, ramps, holes, slingshots) clocking up points; the memory storing the position of the ball; the players; and finally, the specific combinations each time a target is hit.

Pinball machines are anthropomorphic!

The slightest glitch in the thousands of connections can send the poor pinball machine out of control, and locating it can take anywhere from a few minutes to several hours. With a great deal of patience and a little help from the good old Internet, Double-Click manages to overcome the hurdles and restore the ailing machines to working order.

***

<u>Dark Matter</u>

"Hello there, it's Double-Click's brain again. Speaking of relays and electrical wires, I realize that I forgot to explain how I communicate with the rest of the body. So, once again and with the precious help of the BSI, let me reveal myself to you.

"My neurons communicate with each other via electrical signals called nerve impulses (or action potentials). Each neuron consists of a cell body and extensions called dendrites and axons. The latter emit connections with other neurons through terminals which look like small vesicles. These terminals constitute the synapses. My nerve impulse travels down the axon to the synaptic terminal. The more frequent the impulse, the more chemicals the neuron produces: they are my neurotransmitters. These can activate or inhibit the neighboring neuron. I use several types of neurotransmitters: some, like glutamate, are excitatory, others are inhibitory (such as GABA). I have already told you about the most famous ones: dopamine, serotonin, histamine, and acetylcholine. My dopamine-producing neurons are located in a deep region of the brain called the Dark Matter. They are essential to body movement control.

"Sounds simple, doesn't it? All you have to do is find the short circuit. Well, keep on exploring me if you may, dear researchers, I shall be happy to oblige."

38. <u>THE ARCHITECT'S INNARDS</u>

So, what progress did our researchers make so far? A major debate is being waged among the scientific community. Did Double-Click's disease initiate in his brain or his intestines?

***

Son of P...arkin, the Mind-boggling Blog

<u>Old Hubert and The Mad Cow</u>

A Finnish study has recently established a groundbreaking link between the composition of the gut microbiota and Parkinson's disease. Researchers and practitioners at the University Hospital of Helsinki and Hyvinkää analyzed the fecal microbiome of 72 healthy adults and 72 Parkinson's sufferers. They found that the latter had 77.6% less bacteria from the Prevotellaceae family compared to their healthy counterparts.

"Fecal microbiome, hmm, I see," said Double-Click as the line-6 aerial metro train in which he was sitting opened its doors at Station Cambronne.

Researchers are still trying to determine whether the changes observed in the gut microbiota are permanent and linked to the progression of the disease, and therefore with its diagnosis.

Could Double-Click be suffering from a prion disease, like your average mad cow?

Most neurodegenerative diseases, including Alzheimer's, Parkinson's, and amyotrophic lateral sclerosis, share common characteristics with prion diseases.

Time for the Prion Prayer. Even if that sounds a bit prying. Anything, so long as the researchers find what they're looking for.

***

Cambronne found Sir James Parkinson's rebellion against his pathological repute impressive. He who had been unfailingly loyal to the Emperor, who was wounded on several occasions during his campaigns, and who commanded the vanguard of the army during the Hundred Days, shared the injustice of a sidetracked posterity.

Yes, he led the last of the Old Guard in Waterloo. No, he did not respond "The Guard dies, it does not surrender!" when General Colville summoned him to surrender. He couldn't have said it, since he did not die, and actually surrendered.

Ask him if he really did say the five-letter French word meaning poop, the infamous 'Merde', and he'll erupt in anger. But the English think otherwise. They did everything to capture him alive, considering that killing a man like him would have been an insult to his courage.

This anachronistic swearword was definitively attributed to him by Victor Hugo in *Les Misérables* twenty years after his death, in 1862: *'To make that reply and then perish, what could be grander? For being willing to die is the same as to die; and it was not this man's fault if he survived after he was shot. [...] The winner of Waterloo was Cambronne. To thunder forth such a reply at the lightning flash that kills you is to conquer.'*

Thanks to this very beautiful prose, his name comes to mind whenever we think of the Word he said. It too deserves to be rehabilitated; it deserves a new lease of life. Enough is enough. *Merde alors*!

Cambronne is at peace now, dignified and proud in his wrath. Double-Click could easily have heeded the siren song of caricature.

39. <u>THE STARES</u>

A year after the diagnosis, Macha took Double-Click to Japan for a week to take his mind off his recent alliance with Old Hubert. She had organized the trip in secret, for him, their two sisters, and herself. During the few days and nights they spent in Japan, Double-Click was the baby of the family again.

Kyoto/Tokyo
Past/Present
Kimono/Gothik
Present, my sister's priceless gift
In the Far East.
Three sisters, three hearts at the center…
Joy and laughter…
Pure glee, no division…
I, immersed in blissful regression…
Fleetingly a baby again…
Gothik/Kimono
Present/Past.

Tokyo/Kyoto.

***

Back in Paris, Double-Click rereads The Temple of the Golden Pavilion to try and understand the hype around what is now a soulless monument.

"I'd forgotten how boring the crazy monk story was," he tells Aure.

He struggles through another page. Then, a sentence by Mishima jumps at him:

'The disabled, like pretty women, are tired of being stared at; they are sick of living in the eyes of others. And when they stare back, it is with the weight of their very existence.'

Wow, thinks Double-Clicks. This unlikely yet objective-sounding alliance is quite tempting. What would pretty women make of this, I wonder?

***

Intrigued by Mishima's quote – now the subject of debates in the family – César asks his aunt and godmother Olga how a beautiful woman feels when a man looks at her. Is it really as bothersome as when people stare, half curious, half compassionate, at someone who's sick or disabled? He is not convinced.

César hopes to find an answer to his question in the following poem by Barbey d'Aurevilly:

> I spent my days looking at her, only her...
> And at night, of my two eyes wide shut
> She was the apple, as I dreamed of her...
> The gaze has the cheek to go where the heart won't dare.
> The gaze, so bold and yet so weak as it peeps
> At the beloved shape under the dress, away from prying eyes.
> Our heart, our hands, and above all our lips;
> We fix them all in one look!

Double-Click knows where his unease comes from now: it's caused by the attitude of strangers who avert their gaze the moment they see him tremble, or struggle to walk.

40. <u>THE MIRROR EFFECT</u>

Double-Click joins his daughter Anaïs in a small candy-pink pastry shop near Madeleine. She recently started working for a major luxury brand whose headquarters are close by.

They often indulge in moments like this, just the two of them. They agree on just about everything and love to talk about Aure and her male offspring.

As the first-born, Anaïs had the brief privilege of being the object of her mother and father's undivided attention. A bygone privilege, long replaced by the birthright of getting to test her parents' educational choices first hand. The current challenge involves introducing her boyfriend, Germignon, to the family. A task not made easy by her three brothers, who see him as their sister's abductor. They reproach Anaïs for her Stockholm syndrome-like attitude: she insists on standing by this stranger in spite of their disapprobation. As for

Anaïs, she thinks her brothers could do with being a bit more open-minded.

The small pastry shop has been run for forty years by a Japanese couple who make the best éclairs and quiches around. In his pristine white apron, the Chef brings them their order, a salmon koulibiac with appetizing golden crust. His right hand starts to tremble uncontrollably as he sets the dish on the table.

Father and daughter exchange a look, then lower their eyes. Double-Click catches himself thinking 'Poor man' – the very reaction he hates others to have towards him. A discrediting, unnecessary, and inappropriate compassion; one that this man, who appears to have learnt to take Bobbing Bob's pranks in his stride, certainly doesn't need. A sheepish Double-Click turns to Anaïs's benevolent, and gently quizzical, smile for comfort.

***

The Chef is now back by the stove in his small corner kitchen, clearing the plates and placing them in the sink.

He is angry at that blond-haired client who stared at him and then looked away. He'll never get used to it.

"The jerk will see what it's like if it happens to him."

41. <u>THE FOX AND THE OTHERS</u>

Aure never wears Nike, unlike Michael J. Fox, the lead actor in *Back to the Future*. Michael J. Fox is a hero to Double-Click, who sees in him the proof that a determined man can move mountains. Didn't he manage to sell the shoes he wore during a cult scene for several thousand dollars?

To support the Michael J. Fox Foundation, Nike auctioned 1,500 replicas of the shoes worn by the actor in the *Back to the Future* trilogy. The first pair sold for 28,170 euros on eBay! But why such a craze?

After hiding his state of health from the world for many years, the actor revealed his encounter with Old Hubert in a 1998 interview with *People*. Then, freed from the burden of pretense, he left the *Spin City* series to launch the Michael J. Fox Foundation in 2000. Dedicated to finding a cure for Parkinson's, the foundation has raised no less than $650 million to date.

Not bad, thought Double-Click. It goes to show great things can still be achieved even when encumbered by Old Hubert.

Come here and let me hug you, dear little Fox. I thought of a scenario for you. Why don't you go back in time and stop us from meeting Old Hubert? Think about it, and come with me, I'd like to introduce you to other companions in misery who, like you, were smart enough not to fall into the trap set by Aki, Bobbing Bob, and Carcan.

Oh, the sense of shame and guilt that makes you want to crawl under the carpet while the three of them play with your nerve center. Not only is your physical and psychological integrity affected, but the people around you bear the brunt of your illness while you try to pretend all is well to the world, when you should be doing the exact opposite: a coming out in due form to reveal your unnatural idyll. Of course, this calls for a good dose of courage; your condition comes with its load of preconceived ideas, as the man who was to become President of the United States of America knew very well.

So, Double-Click set off in search of the heroes who are not afraid to show their true colors, and whose courage he counts on to help him adapt to his own new life. Our psychological constructs need role models. But who are these men and women willing to play scapegoat and publicly embody the disease to free their fellow sufferers of guilt?

Marc Dal Maso

The former French rugby hooker Marc Dal Maso mentioned his pathology in an interview with the newspapers *La Dépêche du Midi* and *Midi Olympique*: '*I suffer from Parkinson's disease*'. With these simple yet powerful words, Marc Dal Maso revealed his secret.

"Ah, so it's a secret, is it?" exclaimed Double-Click. It's top secret, because it is a shameful sin to suffer from an old person's disease when you're young. What pact with the devil did you make to have a life like that of Raphael de César, the young Marquis in Honoré de Balzac's *The Magic Skin*?

Sonya Rykiel

"This disease was my mother's. It damaged her, changed her, tortured her. It's a nasty piece of work lurking behind a very noble name. Parkinson's is a stage name; it's the name of a rose, it's not fit for the sick, that's why I renamed it," she told a weekly newspaper. Double-Click looked up the nickname she gave Old Hubert: '*P de P*' (for 'Putain de Parkinson'). It echoed his own '*Son of P…arkin*'.

François Cavanna

"So that's what the slight – ever so slight! – tremor of the hand is about? The handwriting that goes off at tangents without a word of warning? The eerily confused gait, the sluggish gestures?" Cavanna wrote.

Sylvie Joly

"You can laugh at anything, especially Parkinson's." Sylvie Joly died from this terrible disease in September 2015, at the age of 80. Famous for her sharp wit, the actress received the Molière Award for Best Sketch Show in 1999.

Eureka! Double-Click has found his role model at last – and quite a Joly one too.

***

When the cartoonist Gabs rang the doorbell on the 5th floor of the Boulevard Saint-Germain building, he didn't expect to find such a vast apartment. To be honest, he couldn't quite place Double-Click, for whom he had once drawn professional greeting cards and made quick sketches at a seminar to challenge the long Post-it sessions and other fun-filled events typical of the consulting world.

After inviting Gabs to sit down on one of the long sofas in the spacious living room, Double-Click told him about

Old Hubert, and about his own blog as a way to curb the ailment's growing stranglehold. Then, he asked him if he wouldn't mind illustrating his blog posts. Caught off-guard, Gabs was a little embarrassed by the request.

But Double-Click insisted, and the cartoonist eventually agreed to play along. He made some drawings to help put things into perspective.

Speaking of role models, Gabs told Double-Click about his old friend, the famous French singer Pierre Vassiliu, who was vanquished by Old Hubert. He thought his name ought to appear in Double-Click's list of inspirational sufferers.

The lyrics of Vassiliu's seventies hit song *Qui c'est celui-là?*, somewhere along the lines of 'Who's that funny-looking guy / What's the matter with him?', seemed to echo the stares of commuters who wondered about Double-Click's penguin walk during a recent metro ride.

***

While writing about Michael J. Fox, Double-Click realized that it took the actor several years to reveal his pathology to the public, and that he only did it when he could no longer hide his symptoms.

Fox was right, he thought. To inspire respect rather than fear, one must accept the forced presence of Old Hubert without vanity or pride.

42. <u>ENCOURAGEMENTS</u>

"It could be worse, you could be suffering from Charcot's disease!"

"Would you say you're already experiencing cognitive impairment?"

"Do you want me to tie your shoelaces for you?"

"It's upstairs, but I can take the elevator with you if you want?"

"Don't you want to give alternative medicine a try? All these drugs can't be good for you."

"I read somewhere that anxiety and lack of sleep made the disease worse, you should sleep more and stress less!"

Double-Click has been cohabitating with his illness for six years now, and despite the growing hindrance, he still manages to lead a so-called 'normal' life. That's why he loves to hear the encouragements, at times awkward, of those who know about his predicament and try to comfort him.

So don't hesitate to encourage Double-Click – it does him a world of good.

Oh and by the way, best to avoid this last blunder: "Don't have surgery (Deep Brain Stimulation), I saw a documentary about it on television, the guy turned into a vegetable."

"I was actually considering it. Thanks for that, I'm feeling so much better now!"

43. <u>SCP OR DBS</u>

This morning, Double-Click is having coffee with Ralph, an actuarial consultant who has been working with him for a few years. His job involves calculating how much a thrifty person will have to save to pay for his retirement and that of a spendthrift, based on their respective life expectancies.

Their morning coffee routine was first established six years earlier, when the then 'new hire' consultant and Double-Click were having lunch. As the meal drew to an end, Ralph told Double-Click that both his divorced parents were seriously ill, and that he spent all his free time looking after them. His father suffered from Parkinson's. Double-Click, who was just after being diagnosed himself, chose not to reveal his condition yet, but he asked Ralph many questions about his father to try and get some idea of what to expect in the future.

Double-Click has since told Ralph about his disease. He enjoys their monthly coffees, and listening to Ralph gives him some insight as to what his own children might be going through. Double-Click and Ralph go into details about the disease, its progression, and the benefits of Deep Brain Stimulation on Ralph's father, who was among the first patients to experience this technique more than twenty years ago.

***

Son of P...arkin, the Mind-boggling Blog

Double-Click's Reincarnation as a Blood Pressure Monitor

The French can be proud of discovering the benefits of 'Stimulation Cérébrale Profonde', or 'Deep Brain Stimulation' (sounds better in English) in the treatment of Old Hubert. This technique was empirically discovered by Professor Alim-Louis Benabid in 1987 at the University Hospital of Grenoble. The Inserm classifies it as a major breakthrough.

Read on, it's quite amazing.

Chance:

While operating on a patient's specific thalamus area involved in involuntary movements (as was customary at the time), *the researcher Alim-Louis Benabid noted that the tremors disappeared under high frequency stimulation.*

And audacity:

Alim-Louis Benabid was audacious in that he tested the effect of different frequencies, wrote Professor Pierre Pollak, a Geneva-based neurologist who was working with Alim-Louis Benabid at the time.

Now performed worldwide, this technique is often prescribed when DOPE and its catalysts fail to conceal the visible syndromes. Double-Click has reached a crossroads in the evolution of his condition. The DOPE is still effective, albeit less regularly, thus subjecting him to painful 'Off' periods when he least expects it.

But he's not certain he wants to have his skull trepanned. Yes, that's how it's called. Like any other technique, it can fail, or the result can be disappointing – even downright ineffective. Of course, the fact that this technique gives spectacular results in most cases is worth considering. Fatigued by his indecision, Double-Click hopes things will seem clearer in the morning. As he drifts off to sleep, he imagines his beloved Aure hitting buttons on a remote control that commands the electrodes freshly implanted in his dark matter to turn him into a drone, a vacuum cleaner, even a blood pressure monitor.

Sure, women run the world, but hopefully not to the point of wanting to turn their husbands into mere connected devices. Mind you, if Double-Click had no choice in the matter, he would probably rather be a blood pressure monitor. This way, at least, he would get to squeeze Aure's arm from time to time.

***

Antonin had a strange dream last night. He was in the practical work room of his preparatory class, but instead of being with by his classmates, he was surrounded by researchers of all ages and nationalities. No one seemed to be following a particular method. There were teams all over the place, doing their own thing. A game of Monopoly was displayed on the floor that looked like a giant plasma screen. The iconic banker in the top hat was handing out dollar bills at random to the most active-looking teams. Suddenly, he turned to Antonin, who felt out of place and wanted to run away – but his legs refused to obey him. The banker's moustache started to blink, alternating from white to red while he advanced towards a petrified Antonin. The man suddenly brandished his cane, cursing, almost touching the boy.

The plasma screen fell black; then it turned into a tilted pinball machine board on which Antonin began to slide. He immediately recognized the Black Hole, Double-Click's eighteenth pinball machine. The banker fell. He now looked like Antonin's Russian teacher. Oblivious to the danger, he slid towards a bumper and was sent hurtling back into the unfathomable depths of the universe. The Black Hole was not just a game after all.

Antonin was safe now. The lab was white again, and empty. Then Double-Click appeared. He needed him to fix a jukebox. He brandished large technical diagrams which meant nothing to Antonin.

Professor Shadoko joined them. He was very small. Antonin scooped him up in his hand. He was shouting double-Dutch words. Antonin stroked his head. The Professor calmed down and mouthed something to Double-Click, who was crouched, unmoving, in front of the jukebox. Antonin finally understood what the little man was trying to say: two wires were hanging out at the back of Double-Click's head. Antonin swiftly reconnected them. There was a spark and Double-Click started moving again. He was now pulling on an endless nylon thread, smiling broadly at Antonin. There was a beautiful siren-shaped fishing lure at the other end of the thread.

Antonin was happy to wake up, and happy he could fix Double-Click.

44. <u>BEWARE OF THE GORILLA</u>

Double-Click was surfing the web, throwing questions at Google – potentially deceptive like a modern-day Pythia – with basic but effective keywords: *Parkinson news, Parkinson breakthrough, Parkinson research*, etc.

As we saw earlier, many a study have been conducted about Old Hubert. But it's a bit like Gaston Lagaffe trying to get Aimé De Mesmaeker to sign contracts – they must absolutely succeed, and yet they invariably fail.

Double-Click had pinned his hopes on so many studies that he learned to read between the lines and tell the serious ones from the blind alleys. That evening, on September 18, 2017, the day before Max's birthday, the 'Parkinson news' query yielded the following top-of-the-page result:

Parkinson's: Monkeys recover their motor functions after receiving a human stem cell transplant.

Lured by the appealing prospect of recovering his motor function, even simian ones, Double-Click read on.

***

Son of P…arkin, the Mind-boggling Blog

<u>Between the Lines</u>

Human stem cells have improved the ability of monkeys with Parkinson's disease to move, according to a study published Wednesday in the journal Nature. *[…] The researchers reprogrammed human adult cells into induced pluripotent stem cells (IPSCs).*

Let's figure out what this means.

'Form of Parkinson's': A form only very partially related to the human forms that already cover a very broad spectrum.

'Promising study': Especially for monkeys…

'IPSCs' (Induced pluripotent stem cells): sounds classier as an acronym, the following words seep into your consciousness: serious, novel, complex. In a word, science with a capital $.

Moving on:

'The monkeys have become more active, they move faster and more easily': would the same effects have been observed had they taken Guronsan or vitamin C?

'As no tumor appeared as a result of the treatment, [...] this confirms the efficacy and safety of the cells used': wow, they almost seem surprised! Double-Click certainly won't be a candidate for clinical trials! He'd rather be in the company of good Old Hubert that with Saint Peter or Satan, depending on the merits, either one of whom he's bound to meet one day anyway.

Beware of the Gorilla, concluded Double-Click.

***

It's interesting to point out here that the gorilla was rewarded with a laminated representation of himself that projects a different image depending on the viewing angle. Once the surprise effect wore off, the gorilla observed them all and retained only one. Tilting it to one angle shows King Kong at the top of the Empire State Building; looking at it from the right reveals a biplane flying around an angry King Kong; and rotating the picture about sixty degrees displays King Kong holding the crushed biplane in his triumphant fist. These are called lenticular flip images. They result from the superposition of two distinct visuals printed on lenticular paper.

***

Going over his post again, Double-Click wonders why on earth he chose to digress on lenticular flip images. As it happens, ever since he was a child, he's found these two-way images fascinating. One subject, two visions, either opposing or complementary. Two takes on the same character, increased twofold.

45. <u>GENES AND DISCOMFORT</u>

Could genetic analysis have predicted such duplication? This is clearly an essential question. Understanding what causes the evolution of disease-specific genes is necessary in order to treat them. This, in any case, is the great challenge of gene therapy.

***

Son of P...arkin, the Mind-boggling Blog

<u>Spaghetti or Linguine</u>

Double-Click decides to take a closer look at his own odd-sounding genes, since their mutation may well be the root cause of his daily discomfort. The most common ones are: alpha-synuclein, LRRK2, Parkin, DJ-1, PINK1, or the more recent VPS13C involved in an early and severe form of the disease. There may be many more, but these are the most relevant to our topic.

Double-Click is not a geneticist; he only has a limited understanding of these transformations. He focuses in particular on alpha-synuclein, whose name reminds him of *Target Alpha* – one of his favorite pinball machines.

Alpha-synuclein is a protein of the synuclein family that in recent years has become one of the most observed proteins by researchers. Beneficial in its normal configuration but toxic in its fibrillar form, this 'double agent' seems to play an essential role in the disruption of the neuronal system.

Hang on – this blog's getting way too serious! Keep this up, Double-Click, and we'll go straight to the next chapter, where we heard a cult video on L-Dopa is playing.

"Bear with me, I'm getting to the point," temporizes Double-Click. "Researchers are people like you and me at the end of the day, they love Italian cuisine too."

A Franco-Belgian team, including researchers from the Institut des neurosciences Paris Saclay (CNRS/Université Paris-Sud), has identified two specific forms of the fibers in this molecule, shaped like 'linguine' and 'spaghetti', and proven that they cause Parkinson's disease and multi-system atrophy (MSA) respectively.

Spaghetti and linguine in the brain. Wow. *Endless pastabilities*, he thought. What more will they discover? White sauce in dark matter?

***

Old Hubert has summoned Aki, Bobbing Bob, and Carcan. They are holding their annual symposium to assess what might jeopardize research and eradicate potential threats. For the first time, a journalist has managed to sneak in among the participants. As the speakers take turns at the rostrum, he realizes that there isn't just one Old Hubert, but probably several dozen of them. They're all related, but not to the point of being Siamese – or even normal – twins. No, as it turns out there are quite different, be it in their facial features, their body shape, their gestures, their gait. Take a closer look and you'll see.

It's hard to summarize a whole day of presentations in just a few lines, but here's an overview. After thousands of years of absolute tranquility, the living conditions of Old Hubert and his coterie have changed dramatically. It all began two centuries ago, when Sir James Parkinson produced the first map of their secret territory. The cartographic details showed an imprecise toponymy of their organization, but for the first time, their existence had been revealed. They didn't think it would go any further at first. The missions deployed to characterize them were conducted by very serious people – albeit with rudimentary technologies. It was like trying to take a picture of an atom using the daguerreotype technique. But technologies have made great progress over the past twenty years. Electron microscopes operating in transmission or reflection mode, with or without scanning, produce increasingly accurate images. And things are fast evolving. It's only a matter of time before

they are found and eradicated – and they know it.

Meanwhile, Double-Click's Old Hubert comes to his own conclusions: *'I'm sick of constantly having to find new hideouts, new jamming systems and whatnot. To be honest, if I could communicate with these researchers I'd give them a couple of useful tips. Of course, I'd expect a well-deserved retirement in return.'*

A redeemed Old Hubert – who would have thought it?

46. <u>IN FAVOR OF RETIREMENT AT 60</u>

Son of P...arkin, the Mind-boggling Blog

<u>My Wild Night with L-Dopa</u>

They walk into a vast room adorned with huge windows overlooking the Grand Canal. They contemplate the sun sinking into the lagoon, shining its last rays on the throngs of tourists who came to admire the daily communion between the earth and its star. A quotidian spectacle of endless variations, on a loop for billions of years. A few logs are burning in the baroque fireplace whose blackened bricks contrast with the pink stucco pillars that frame it.

L-Dopa slowly slides the top of her blouse off her shoulder, revealing a streak of freckles on her creamy white skin.

How far do these milky ways go? wonders Double-Click as he draws near her.

Hold it, dear hero, this is none of our business. You forgot to put on your patch again, and now your brain's playing tricks on you.

***

At nearly sixty years of age, L-Dopa is a true miracle of nature. She has not aged a bit and still looks as slender as a young girl. Her playful yet determined character is as alluring as ever, and quite irresistible. She never complains, but if you only knew her working conditions, you'd realize how dedicated she is – hers is a true calling indeed. She works every day of the year from 7 am till 11 pm – sometimes starting as early as five in the morning. No days off, no vacations. She only ever gets a break when we forget to call on her. That happens four, maybe five times a year at the most. In short, after years of being in the spotlight – and enjoying it – L-Dopa is looking forward to a well-deserved retirement. She has done her fair share of the work, but now she wonders if it was all in vain.

"I've had a great professional life, but the time has come for me to focus on my family."

47. <u>UNDERCOVER VS UNTOUCHABLE</u>

Double-Click would rather take the metro than any other means of transport. It's always been the case, and it's not about to change; the mayor of his city has unilaterally decided to transform the streets of Paris into a giant mousetrap and the bus lanes into death rows for fearless cyclists. And so we join Double-Click on his favorite metro line.

Known as the 'aerial line', Line 6 offers a breathtaking view of Paris, uncluttered by traffic jams from the top decker, until it goes underground at Station Pasteur. A good opportunity for Double-Click to share his idea with us, about developing vaccines to fend off the mutation of alpha-synuclein into poisoned pasta, spaghetti or linguini – whatever takes Old Hubert's fancy.

***

Son of P...arkin, the Mind-boggling Blog

<u>Vaccines</u>

Double-Click has found two biotechs that are working on the subject via two different techniques.

Passive immunotherapy is the administration of laboratory-produced antibodies to patients. The purpose of these antibodies is to identify and bind to mutated alpha-synucleins, in order to help the body eliminate them.

A great way to dismantle the Undercover Pasta Gang.

Active immunotherapy aims to boost the immune system so that it can detect these abnormalities and produce antibodies to eliminate them.

A different approach, closer to the formation of an elite corps such as The Untouchables.

Double-Click, who's an investigation buff, volunteered for the second option. He wouldn't mind playing the part of Eliot Ness, but his hopes are crushed by the answer:

'Dear Patient, dear Caregiver,

*If the development of our vaccine is successful, a study physician from your region will contact you **in a few years from now**.'*

Double-Click never heard from them again.

He had no choice but to continue his research.

48. <u>LADIES AND GENTLEMEN</u>

Teams of researchers from all over the world are quite fond of sensational announcements. Double-Click, who initially attributed them to the discoverer's pride,' soon realized they're nothing but marketing tricks, and that these so-called great advances were just one of the techniques used to promote a fast-developing business called fundraising.

***

Son of P…arkin, the Mind-boggling Blog

<u>Charity Begins at Home</u>

'Fundraising relies on marketing, communication, and strategic management techniques, as well as strong ethics and interpersonal skills among other things.'

This says it all. On the metro taking him home, Double-Click closes the website page.

He'd decided to take Line 8 via Station Bonne Nouvelle, where superstition invariably drives him to check *Parkinson's news* on his phone, on his way to Station Gaîté.

He changes trains at Invalides, which has perforce become 'his' station. A familiar complaint rises between Duroc and Montparnasse that irritates or moves, depending on the commuters' mood:

"Sorry to bother you, ladies and gentlemen, my name is Cosinus. I lost my job as a researcher because I never found anything. I know you're sick of people like me harassing you and believe me, I'm not enjoying this either, seeing the way you stare at me, but have you got any spare change? No, actually, forget it. How about a metro ticket? What's the point, I never pay anyway. A lunch voucher? A contactless card? A Rolex? A job in Parliament? Anything to help me stay clean and eat proper meals and sleep in a real bed..."

Double-Click realizes that fundraising happens at every level. The ground rules are pretty simple: it's all about attracting attention and turning it – and here's the rub – into compassion, i.e. hard cash.

This gets Double-Click thinking. Wouldn't it be great if a positive review helped him win his very own award?

'*Son of P...arkin* is by far the best Parkinson's blog out there. Funny, well-documented, and engaging, it hooks you from the first sentence and only releases you after the last post.' Double-Click daydreams about receiving his award to thunderous applause as the enthralled audience gives him a standing ovation.

***

This morning, he and Aure are having breakfast on the black granite kitchen countertop. The bow window overlooks the rooftops of the Ministry for the Ecological and Solidary Transition. Sounds promising!

This is their 'us-time', when they can have a chat, just the two of them, over a cup of tea. Aure confides in Double-Click that she finds him more and more distant, in his own world.

"I'm not the only one to think so," she adds. "The children are worried, too. Is there something wrong? You spend hours in front of your computer. Sometimes you get up in the middle of a meal to go to your office, as if driven by some irrepressible inspiration. I'm not even sure you remember what you were eating when that happens."

To her surprise, Double-Click does not elude the question: "I am very disturbed by the way I feel about myself, and how people see me, since my symptoms have become obvious. I want to find a way to reinstate Sir James Parkinson's name, I mean, so that it's not just used in a degrading way. When Charcot named the disease after its discoverer, he wanted to pay tribute to him. Similarly, Alois Alzheimer was allotted the infamous memory-loss disease by a man called Emil Kraepelin in

Clinical Psychiatry. But today, if you say 'I have Parkinson's' or 'I have Alzheimer's' to someone, they immediately imagine you taking line 2 from Étoile (a fleeting tribute to the unknown patient you've suddenly become) to go to Père-Lachaise cemetery via Couronnes. And your family realize they will go straight from Station Liberté on line 8 to Rue des Boulets on line 9, without changing at Bonne Nouvelle. I want to understand what makes people react that way, and I want to change it."

49. <u>THE RESEARCHERS AND THE GURU</u>

Lost in his thoughts, Double-Click realizes he forgot to mention all the molecules that are already on the market. As these remedies don't require a new authorization, they're available almost immediately.

That's what happened to Viagra. Originally developed to treat angina pectoris, it came to serve other purposes.

As for Parkinson's, a discovery in particular raised hope:

A drug used to treat leukemia was found to improve cognitive and motor functions in Parkinson's sufferers.

The Lazarus effect was in motion, and the first results were nothing short of miraculous.

Researchers reported that a chairbound patient was able to walk again, and that three patients who had lost the ability to speak can now hold conversations.

Needless to say, the switchboard at Georgetown University was flooded with calls when the announcement was made, to such an extent that three students got slightly injured. But other researchers soon questioned the results of an experiment that had been conducted on only eleven patients. That's the last we heard of it. Lazarus had crawled back into his grave.

A diabetes medication seemed to fit the bill too:

A drug initially designed to treat patients with type 2 diabetes appears to slow the progression of Parkinson's disease.

And more recently, another drug initially intended to treat asthma:

Sometimes, certain drugs are found to have unexpected effects. This is the case with salbutamol, a molecule used in the treatment of asthma which, according to a recent study, also appears to be effective against Parkinson's.

What is there to say about all these miracle cures that surge out of nowhere, only to prove disappointing in the end? Double-Click turns to his favorite proverb once again: 'Keep trying and you'll get there in the end. The more you fail, the more chances you have to succeed.'

It will work, thinks Double-Click. How else could it be? *Any guru out there to enlighten me?*

***

Double-Click had another strange dream in which his father, Odette's husband – nicknamed Shanghai by his brothers-in-law for some obscure reason – returned from beyond the grave to deliver a message to him. Although the man was severe and authoritarian, Double-Click feels a pang in his heart as he fondly recalls him overflowing with demanding love towards his three sisters and himself.

He appeared Snapchat-style on the screen of his smartphone and said: "Nothing is permanent in this world, not even our troubles." Then he vanished before Double-Click could take a screenshot. And now his father's quote, borrowed from Charlie Chaplin, rings in his ears like a strange premonition.

***

"The brain is not like the prostate!" exclaimed Professor Y.

Although Double-Click never gave it much thought before, he wasn't sure he agreed with this truism. But he didn't want to risk vexing Professor Y.

Funnily enough, just as Double-Click was wondering about the changes yet to come in his life due to his pathology, the Research Institute to which he regularly made donations invited him to meet the one person most apt to answer the questions that burdened him about future therapeutic approaches. He gladly accepted the invitation, in the company of his twin sister Aure. Professor Y is to Old Hubert what the Pope is to the Catholic Church. This is no innocent comparison, since John Paul II was partially canonized (if I may say so) for miraculously curing a sufferer of this pathology.

Professor Y is an open and considerate man whose extraordinary personality and brilliant mind outshine his agreeable demeanor. He is capable of dazzling insights as well as sustained and profound thinking.

Listening to him fills Double-Click with a deep respect. He truly admires this man whose supreme intelligence makes accessible subjects that are usually out of reach for most of us. In the space of half an hour, Professor Y proposes three lines of reflection that enlighten and structure Double-Click's profuse and confused cogitations about his pathology. He immediately transfers them onto *Son of P...arkin*.

***

Son of P...arkin, the Mind-boggling Blog

<u>Where Are We Now?</u>

"Old Hubert is not unique, it is plural. Many individuals are hiding behind the one mask, perhaps thirty or so," ventures Professor Y. "They materialize according to genetic and environmental criteria. Moreover, the disease has already been classified, notably in accordance with the genes PARK-1, PARK-2, PARK-3, PARK-4, PARK-11, and so on."

This is how Old Hubert and his Siamese twins, each with their own specificities, trick researchers into contradictory interpretations. There isn't one single defense strategy. Future therapy will certainly involve a combination of treatments instead of one universal and miraculous drug.

"The brain represents the challenge of the infinitesimally mall, just as the universe represents that of the infinitely large. It is the next boundary to cross in medical research. The challenge is huge. Teams around the world are regularly publishing papers on the discovery, the role, or the mutations of a gene involved in the pathology.

"The battle against neurodegenerative diseases joins forces with the fight against aging. It is the Holy Grail of human research. The billions spent on advertising to promote the so-called age-reversal properties of cosmetics and food products almost had us believe it could be true. But in reality, no treatment, product, or ointment has ever slowed the aging of a cell. And what is true for aging in general is also true for neurodegenerative diseases in particular."

Anyway, if it really were that simple, there wouldn't be any bald men left on the planet, thought Double-Click, incidentally noting that the golf courses that ran along his receding hairline expanded from 9 to 18 holes in just a few years. If aging joins forces with diseases like Parkinson's, it's easy to see why research in these fields is as complex as it is essential.

***

Just as he is about to publish his post, Double-Click is seized with a dizzy spell of such magnitude it could have been induced by standing at the top of Tokyo's Sky Tree – had he climbed it. He no longer thinks of his illness as a common pathology; he now sees it as a form of accelerated aging – an all-encompassing condition rather than an isolated ailment. *Old Hubert might just remain a mystery for quite some time yet*, ponders Double-Click, a bit stunned by the multitude of new questions engendered by his interview with Professor Y.

He gets so immersed in thought that he falls asleep, lulled by the rocking Shinkansen train (connecting Tokyo to Kyoto, the cities with inverted syllables). And soon he dreams, something about the police of every country in the world joining forces to arrest the Old Hubert gang.

50. <u>GOOD AND EVIL</u>

After their meeting with Professor Y, Aure was feeling enthusiastic. His explanations had been so easy to follow. Playful, she asked Double-Click:

"Any food for thought in this for you, darling?"

He looked at her, amused.

"Oh yes, big time. It's made me realize that I don't need to worry about how others see me anymore. I can just focus on being me. I think I'll make a major contribution to my blog: a 'plea for the rehabilitation of Sir James Parkinson' that will reach beyond the current symbols of this pathology."

What was this plea about? Double-Click explained:

"I believe that the fear associated with the names Alzheimer's and Parkinson's is not just a coincidence. It embodies our collective fear of aging and death. And the connection pointed out by the professor between aging and neurodegenerative diseases hit home. It helped me put my thoughts in order.

"Parkinson's is the progressive loss of motor skills control; with Alzheimer's, the loss pertains to reasoning and memory. This is obviously a simplified definition.

"No one wants to be confronted with the demise of human balance or with the harmonious communion between body and mind. These two diseases carry within them the renunciation of an ideal consubstantial with mankind. This is why it's so hard for the sufferers and their families to accept the diagnosis. It also explains why these diseases trigger such violent rejection. Just look at how Trump considers them. But in the case of Parkinson's, motor complications don't stop people from living a normal life during many years, except in certain forms that progress much faster. Just look at what Michael J. Fox did after he was diagnosed. He achieved a lot more than the vast majority of healthy people ever will.

"Hence, there is a discrepancy between the sufferer who, despite his disease and the very real difficulties he faces, doesn't give up his family and social life, and the way people generally perceive his or her condition. In addition, the moment a serious illness is diagnosed, the sufferer loses all hope of being eternal. But, having to face their own mortal reality, they develop a lucid vision of the future and its uncertainties, and in a certain way, they learn to appreciate the beauty of the 'here and now'. Their emotions are heightened as they experience every little thing more intensely. They develop a stronger connection to the world and are more receptive to it.

"To quote Alexandre Dumas, 'How so, Monsieur?' said Mazarin, 'I do not understand you.' 'I mean, Monseigneur, that years of suffering count twice over, and that I have been for twenty years a sufferer.'

"Don't get me wrong, I'm not suggesting that anyone should fall ill just to experience the present more intensely. The healthy have great privileges that I would have liked to keep, had I been given the choice."

Aure didn't dare interrupt him. Her Double-Click had been conceptualizing situations well before he met Old Hubert. And whenever the mood took him he would retreat into his mind, surrounded by his thoughts in consistory mode, only to emerge when his brain expelled a swirl of white smoke.

"What do you mean by rehabilitating Sir James Parkinson or Alois Alzheimer?"

Double-Click had been expecting this question:

"Well, the primary response is to kill the bearer of bad news. How can that be avoided? This urge is not new, as attested by many famous examples. In Sophocles's *Antigone*, 'No one loves the messenger who brings bad news'; in Shakespeare's *Antony and Cleopatra*, 'The nature of bad news infects the teller'; and, more explicitly, in Friedrich Schiller's *Cassandra*:

Veil my mind once more in slumbers Let me

heedlessly rejoice; Never have I sung glad numbers

Since I've been thy chosen voice. Knowledge of the

future giving, Thou hast stolen the present day, Stolen the moment's joyous living,-- Take thy false gift, then, away!

When Alois Alzheimer autopsied his patient, he showed that the pathology is linked to the deterioration of certain areas of the brain. And when Alois Alzheimer and James Parkinson described and characterized the diseases they uncovered, they actually 'invented' them. From then on, these pathologies were no longer the consequence of a curse or of the mere erosion of time; they became diseases in their own right, identifiable through a diagnosis based on specific clinical signs.

"So, you're saying that Alzheimer, Parkinson, Charcot, Huntington, Creutzfeldt, and Jacob, to name only them, were condemned to share their name with the disease they discovered in punishment for their discovery?" asked Aure.

"All I'm saying is, they were de facto the bearers of bad news and, coincidence or not, their name was attributed to their discovery. They were thus condemned to bear the name of their own discovery forever. When I looked them up, I read that Hippocrates had perhaps sensed the danger of negative anachronistic posterity. When he compared breast cancer to a lump surrounded by elongated streaks reminiscent of the legs of a crab (Latin for cancer), he left no room for his discovery to be named after him. Hippocrates went on to become the father of medicine, and not the symbol of cancer. No one will ever die from a breast Hippocrates or a liver Hippocrates."

"But what's the point of rehabilitating them?"

"Well, for one, to pay tribute to their work. Their findings led the scientific community to develop treatments for the diseases they uncovered. And by rehabilitating the symbol, you rehabilitate everyone in its wake. In other words, all the sufferers.

"The patients are the children of Parkinson's and Alzheimer's. The bearers of the bad news, if you like. As sufferers of the disease, they embody a potential twist of fate no one wants to consider – especially not their friends and family. They once were healthy and normal, like I once was too, and out of the blue they become the living proof that Parkinson's can strike anyone. It's quite destabilizing, don't you think?"

"Aren't you exaggerating a bit?"

"No, it's just human, all too human. It's a natural defense reaction. There's no getting away from it! I would have reacted that way too in the same situation. Today, all chronic patients bring bad news to the people around them, as their condition inherently suggests that anyone can be affected too."

A brief silence, then:

"Have you ever heard of the lenticular flip effect?" Double-Click asked.

Aure gave him a knowing look. He smiled:

"When you look at me, you don't see the two images of King Kong, before and after he crushed the plane. When you look at me, you see a Click who turned into a

Double-Click one day. For twenty-five years, my image evolved with fashion and the passing years, by your side. When the diagnosis hit, a second image superimposed itself on the first one, inconspicuous, drawn with invisible ink: it was Double-Click's image. The early days were reassuring, you could still see Click, it was the same image you had been gazing at all these years through your right eye. Of course, you were a bit apprehensive at the thought of glimpsing Double-Click through your left eye, but for a long time both images overlapped almost perfectly. And then, little by little, the hidden image started to live a life of its own. The multifold symptoms made visible the invisible ink and revealed the silhouette of the sufferer: Double-Click. And over the months, his image became increasingly conspicuous to the point of being omnipresent and distorting the original image of Click into oblivion.

"Rehabilitating Sir James Parkinson is akin to acknowledging the neurologist, and not the 'disease of' that lurks behind his name. Rehabilitating the patient entails looking at Click through your right eye even though Old Hubert strives to rivet your left eye onto Double-Click's symptoms. This leads to a shared feeling of guilt between the sufferer, who projects an unwanted image of himself, and the beholder who glimpses it with his left eye despite his pledge to never open it."

Aure listened attentively to Double-Click. She was relieved that he chose to open up to her with such clear-sightedness about the profound changes in their relationship. Deep down, she acknowledged the complexity, sometimes the contradiction, of her own feelings. Her Double-Click had sensed it for a long time but hadn't been able to put it into words until now, for he was immersed in his own self-esteem or lack thereof, his anger at Old Hubert, and his difficulty with his wife's right to feel attractive. Aure's childhood secret had long subjected her to the discomfort of ambivalent feelings and of being wrongly accused. Her background predisposed her to be acutely aware of the damage caused by mutual guilt, the kind that undermines interpersonal relationships regardless of their initial strength.

They smiled at each other as they recalled the anxious look, portending trials to come, they had exchanged when Double-Click turned fifty-one. The first day, not so long ago, of their new life.

51. <u>FIFTY-ONE</u>

In truth, Double-Click has no memory of his fifty-first birthday, on that Tuesday in May 2011. Aure and the children had probably baked a chocolate cake. There must have been gifts, too. They probably had dinner on the rectangular, tablecloth-covered wooden table in the dining room, rather than on the round aluminum table in the kitchen.

There must have been a lot of laughter. Anaïs was soon turning nineteen, and César seventeen. Antonin had celebrated his thirteenth birthday the previous Saturday, and Max still had to wait until September for his eleventh birthday. Aure was forty-six.

While they were having dinner, did he think about his phone conversation with Irina, when he'd told her he wanted to know? He couldn't tell. It had been his last opportunity to bask in the illusion of immortality that used to come so easily to him, and that had remained unscathed despite the many tentative diagnoses. Oh, the power of self-deception when it comes to believing that misfortune only befalls other people! It has spared you for so long now, why would it suddenly change course?

Aure had intuited it, and Click, unbeknownst to himself, had been a carrier. He had seen relatives lose their illusion of immortality in much more dramatic circumstances. He remembered being Antonin's age, spending the weekend at a friend's in Orléans. The doorbell rang. It was Saturday evening. They opened the door, saw two gendarmes, were told to go play somewhere else. The air was eerily tense. They could sense something bad had happened. The next day, Click was still with his friend when someone told the friend that his mother, who had gone skiing for the weekend, would never come back. An avalanche had just shattered his friend's life.

No need to wait fifty-one years to lose one's illusion of immortality. It had happened to his friend when he was just a teenager. That day, Click realized how incredibly lucky he was that his Odette was still alive. He decided that he should never complain again. He also realized that life did not care about being fair. A wave of guilt-ridden and useless compassion engulfed him.

You can lose your illusion of immortality anytime, anywhere. There's no rule. Max Gallo met Old Hubert late in his life. He was over 80 when, confronted with the diagnosis, he declared: 'We believe we are immortal, but we are not.' And yet, he had endured the unfathomable grief of losing his daughter long before that. He too must have perceived the inevitable loss of immortality, but he lacked the proof.

The day after his birthday, when he hung up with Pat, Click the Immortal became Double-Click the Mortal. There was no escaping it. His sisters, who were also facing serious health issues, could testify to this.

And now, a few years on, don't expect Double-Click to pretend it's a good thing. Click lived his life in blissful insouciance; Double-Click is often happy but no longer carefree. What he has lost in casualness, he has gained in insight. He may have lost the ability to look far into the future, but he has learned to appreciate the here and now. He is no longer invincible, but he is all the more humane. He used to like being supportive, now he likes being supported.

The shift from healthy to unhealthy does not end here; it also encompasses the transition from being spontaneous, instinctive, and mechanical to trying harder, overcoming hurdles, focusing, and never giving up. And in Max Gallo's own words, freedom 'is a sensation that fades, since you are no longer free.' Because Old Hubert, like all serious diseases, constantly reminds you that all the things you take for granted actually result from a long learning process: walking, talking, apprehending, standing upright, feeling, sleeping, etc. Nothing is ever a given. To pretend, to mask, to hide symptoms is taxing, it weighs on the mind. This explains why the people around Double-Click think he lives in a world of his own. In its irrepressible course, the metamorphosis profoundly upends one's interactions with other people. To quote the historian once more, 'The disease transforms a writer's relationship with himself, with other writers, and with the world as it is.' His world is transmogrified.

Click is not a writer, and neither is Double-Click. But the latter's heightened sensitivity was stirred to the point of pain by the changes in his relationships, with his wife of course, but also with his father, children, friends, sisters, collaborators. Double-Click would be lying if he said that the upheaval in his relations with others was 'a blessing in disguise', because it carried a lot of frustrations that are sometimes difficult to accept. Still, he finds some truth in the saying.

Would his relationship with Aure and the children have evolved in the same way without Old Hubert? No, but it would have evolved nonetheless, differently, over time. As it had always done. Our connections are like us, alive. Their strength is interdependent with the intensity of our love and affection.

Illness, like other trials, reveals and accelerates our evolution. For years, Double-Click thought it was arbitrary; now he knows it is a part of his life, just like everything that happened to him before. As long as things went his way, he thought he was in control of time. Old Hubert took care of lifting the veil of illusion.

Even if Old Hubert is defeated one day, this revelation will never be undone. The healthy and the unhealthy are indivisible. Click and Double-Click are one. The One in Fifty-One.

Fifty-one – a birthday like no other

EPILOG

Ksar Massa, on the south coast of Morocco – June 2027

The hotel where the consultants in Click's firm had stayed thirty years earlier has just reopened. It's new owners, Hasni, who used to be a photographer, and Clara, a former consultant, have worked hard to make their shared dream come true.

The building, which has been renovated with great taste, blends well with the surrounding landscape. Click contacted Hasni and Clara three months ago to ask if he could rent (?) the hotel. He wanted to celebrate the union of two dear friends who had fought for many years. Clara was overjoyed when she realized the request came from her former boss, back to the days when she worked as a consultant. When they spoke on the phone, he congratulated her on her great achievement. He was happy to return to Ksar Massa. It will be a blast from the past, he said. Back to when he was a consultant.

He inquired about the hotel's facilities and asked for pictures of the venue so he could plan the reception himself. He asked for all the rooms to be equipped with a pinball machine, and booked room number 51 for Aure and himself.

The first guests arrived last night. Clara almost fainted when she recognized the man getting out of the long black limousine. Although he now bears the weight of years, he is still incredibly alluring. Clint E. Junior, a gifted actor-director just like his father, had never set foot in Morocco until now. Spellbound by the beauty of the place, he holds his arm out for Olga to join him. Together, they contemplate the ocean that stretches beyond the cliffs upon which the hotel stands.

Cardinal San Antonio arrived shortly afterwards. He had flown to Agadir from Rome on a commercial flight.

The Cardinal, whose first wedding celebration had been that of his hosts, had feared he might never make it. The conclave for the election of the new Pope had lasted longer than expected. Against all odds, John XXIV – Giovanni to his close circle – was to succeed the late John Paul III.

Clara then welcomed César, now a successful restorer of vintage cars. When she looked at his face, she was troubled to see the expressions of the man who still went by the name of Ludwig some thirty years ago.

Irina and Pat settled in the west wing, which Double-Click had reserved for the health professionals. Their rooms were adjacent to a vast suite whose guests had been kept a mystery – Double-Click was maintaining the suspense. He had told Clara that they would descend from celestial heights, and that there was no need to send someone to pick them up. A few hours later, Alois, James, Jean-Martin, and Hippo were comfortably settled in their suite. Clara didn't even have to open the door for them. They invited their immediate neighbors for drinks before dinner was due to begin. Pat, who had always dreamed of meeting Hippo, had a long chat with him.

Aure is talking with Anaïs about her new job. She wants her professional opinion on the hotel's layout. Anaïs is the manager of a five-star hotel chain that she and her brother Max recently bought from Qataris who lost everything to the solar battery. Meanwhile, Aure is keeping an eye on her nine grandchildren playing in the pool.

The 50th and 51st guests are due to join them later that night. Convincing them to take time off from their golden retirement years hadn't been easy, but they eventually said 'yes' to Double-Click.

The party is about to begin. L-Dopa is sitting at the head table, across from Old Hubert and to the left of Double-Click, himself facing Aure. The mysterious guests finally got married, after fighting for so many years.

Clara and Hasni are standing side by side, proud, as their guests tuck into their starters. Clara watches Aure and Double-Click unfold the pieces of rolled-up paper she prepared. She made sure they picked the same ones — that's what friends are for, after all. Aure and Double-Click read their respective message, and smile.

'An encounter has changed your life.'

SPECIAL THANKS

To Marie-Cécile, my better half, my number one on whom I can always count.

To my children Joséphine, Rodolphe, Auguste, and Basile who never stopped laughing at my jokes, especially when I was the only one to find them funny.

To my father Claude, who died before he could find out I was the Son of Parkin, and not his. Had he been still alive, I bet he wouldn't have let Old Hubert get away with it.

To my dear Odette, my mother, who keeps telling me, "We are lucky in our family, we are never ill," but who worries herself sick at the thought of having perhaps failed my conception. Don't worry, I'm happier than all the children you didn't have.

To my sister, Marie-Odile, a classics teacher – no less! – who has proofread my spelling and syntax, and so much more,

To Valérie, who took over when *Parkinson le glas ?* became *Fifty-one*. I couldn't have done it without her.

To my sisters Marie-Anne and Marie-Claude, who contributed to the diagnosis from behind the scenes and whose affection is a whole lot more effectual than Sinemet,

To Peter Dunlap-Shohl and GABS for kindly accepting to illustrate *Fifty-one*,

To my physiotherapist Slim, my therapist Mona, and my neurologist Dr. Z., whose anonymity has been preserved without their prior consent,

To my reviewers, whose objective opinion I sought while secretly hoping it would be as subjective as possible,

To my friends, who shall remain just that if they buy this book and promote it in return for this dedication,

To Cognizant, my employer, and to my colleagues who are flexible with my timekeeping, who give me time to write, and whose many acts of kindness have been a great source of comfort to me,

To my fellow sufferers, who could have done without the illness,

And to all the others, whom I hereby acknowledge but name not out of respect for their natural discretion.